# GCSE D&T Textiles

## The Revision Guide

The best that money can buy
from the country's leading producer
of revision material.

# Contents

# Contents

Published by Coordination Group Publications Ltd.

*Contributors*:
Martin Chester
Charley Darbishire
Maggie Hughes
Jo Lilley
Tim Major
Cathy Osbond
Alice Shepperson
Charlotte Tweedy
James Paul Wallis
Simon Little

ISBN: 1-84146-793-6

With thanks to Julie Schofield and Fiona Leyman-Fox for the proofreading.

Groovy website: www.cgpbooks.co.uk

Jolly bits of clipart from CorelDRAW
With thanks to Hobkirk Sewing Centre, Blackburn

Printed by Elanders Hindson, Newcastle upon Tyne.

# Design Brief

The process of <u>designing</u> and <u>making</u> something is called '<u>the design process</u>' (gosh). The whole process can take a while — so, like many pineapples, it's usually broken down into smaller <u>chunks</u>.

## The Design Process is Similar in Industry and School

It's no accident that the things you'll have to do for your <u>Design and Technology project</u> are pretty similar to what happens in <u>industry</u>.

1. The best products are those that address a <u>real need</u>.
2. That's why companies spend so much <u>time</u> and <u>money</u> on <u>customer research</u>. The more people there are who would actually <u>use</u> a product, the more chance it stands of being a <u>roaring success</u>.
3. The <u>best</u> ideas for Design and Technology <u>projects</u> are also those that meet a genuine need.

The rest of this section describes a <u>typical design process</u>.
It shows the sort of thing that happens in <u>industry</u> every day.
It also shows the stages you need to go through while you're putting a <u>Design and Technology project</u> together.

## First get your Idea for a New Product

First things first... whether you're working in the research and development department of a multinational company, or you're putting together your GCSE Textiles project, you need to explain <u>why</u> a new product is <u>needed</u>. It could be for one of the following reasons:

1) There are <u>problems</u> with an existing product.
2) The <u>performance</u> of an existing design could be <u>improved</u>.
3) There's a <u>gap</u> in the market that you want to fill.

## The Design Brief explains Why your Product is Needed

The <u>design brief</u> explains <u>why</u> there might be a need for a new product.
It should include the following:

1) An <u>outline</u> of the <u>problem</u> and who it <u>affects</u>.
2) The <u>need</u> arising from the problem.
3) What you <u>intend</u> to do about it (e.g. design and make...).
4) How your product will be <u>used</u>.
5) The <u>environment</u> it will be used in.

**Design Brief for Winter Bikini**

There is no bikini available that is designed for use in cold weather.

So we will manufacture a bikini to meet this need for people who like to sunbathe in the cold.

Basically, the design brief should concentrate on the <u>problem</u> you're trying to <u>solve</u>.

## Remember — your project doesn't have to involve bikinis...

Your design brief should be simple and concise, and allow you room for development. A design brief should <u>not</u> be a detailed description of what you intend to make — you can only say this after you've designed it and tried stuff out. Got that... <u>describe the problem</u> first. The rest comes later.

# Research

Once you've written your design brief.., you can start <u>researching</u> your project.
This is what life is all about.

## Research can help you get Ideas

It's worth doing your research <u>carefully</u> — it can give you loads of <u>ideas</u> for the rest of the design process. The point of doing research is to:

1) check that people will actually <u>want</u> your product (although you might have done this already when you <u>chose</u> your project).

2) find out what makes an existing product <u>good</u> or <u>bad</u> — talk to people who actually use this kind of product, and see what they like or dislike.

3) find out the <u>materials</u>, <u>techniques</u> and <u>equipment</u> that you can use, and how they will affect the manufacturing and selling <u>costs</u>.

4) give you a good starting point for <u>designing</u>.

## There are Different Kinds of Research

You can do <u>different kinds</u> of research. These include:

① **Questionnaires** — to find out people's likes/dislikes and so on. This will help you identify your <u>target group</u> and find out <u>market trends</u> (e.g. what things are becoming more <u>popular</u>).

② **Surveying** — go and look at similar products. You could go to shops, use catalogues or surf the net. Find out what you're <u>up against</u>.

③ **Disassembling a product** (i.e. taking it apart) — this will help you find out how a current product is <u>made</u> and how it <u>works</u>. It could also give you information about different <u>materials</u> and <u>processes</u> used, and how <u>existing</u> products meet the needs of potential users.

④ **Measuring** — to find out the <u>sizes</u> of current products. This might give you an idea of the possible size and shape of <u>your</u> product. You could also do some kind of <u>sensory analysis</u> (e.g. you could see how it tastes, feels, looks and smells).

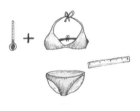

## Research Analysis means Drawing Conclusions

Once you've done your research, you'll need to come to some <u>conclusions</u>. This means deciding how to use the information to help you with your design. This is called <u>research analysis</u>.

Try to do the following:

1) <u>Pick out</u> the useful information.

2) <u>Explain</u> what impact the research will have on your designs.

3) <u>Suggest</u> ways forward from the research gathered.

By the time you've done all this, you should have some ideas about how to tackle your project.

## <u>I disassembled my dog — he doesn't work any more...</u>

Research is important. Trust me. More important at this stage than wearing bikinis or freezing your nose off. And one more thing while I'm ranting... you could also spend some time doing 'book research', e.g. finding out about any British or European standards your product will have to meet.

# Design Specification

Once you've picked out the main points of your research, you're ready to put together a
design specification. So put that lard away... you're not ready to do anything practical yet.

## The Design Specification is a List of Conditions to Meet

The design specification describes the restrictions and possibilities of the product.
It's a good point to start from when you get round to doing the more creative stuff.

1)  The design specification gives certain conditions that the finished product will have to meet.
    Try to put your specification together in bullet form as specific points, rather than a paragraph of explanations.

> E.g. if your research tells you that people would never buy a
> winter bikini that costs more than £100, then your design specification
> might include the statement, "Must cost £100 or less."

2)  Once you've come up with a design, you need to compare it to the specification and confirm that each
    point is satisfied.

    E.g. If your design specification contains these two
    points, then all of your designs should cost no more
    than £100 and not be dark brown on the outside.

    > "The maximum product cost will be £100."
    > "The product should be brightly coloured."

3)  Some points might be harder to compare to your specification simply by looking at the product.

    > E.g. "The product should be comfortable to wear."

    For this, you'll need to get someone to test
    the product once it's been made/modelled.

4)  Include points to describe some or all of the following:

    1.  A description of how it should look
    2.  Details about how it will be used
    3.  Materials, equipment and production method
    4.  Details of size/shape
    5.  Safety points to consider
    6.  Financial constraints

## You might need to make More Than One Specification

You'll probably need to produce several specifications as your project develops:

> Initial Design Specification — this is your first design specification.
> It should be done after your research analysis.

1)  As you develop your design, you'll probably want to make some changes to your design
    specification. This is fine, as long as your design brief is being met and you have taken your
    research analysis into account.

2)  Maybe as a result of some of your modelling (see page 5) you'll find that certain materials
    aren't suitable. You can add this information to an updated specification.

3)  You can keep doing this until you end up with a final product specification.

## I'd never buy a summer bikini...

If I told you that design specifications were going to get your pulse racing, you'd probably suspect I was lying.
And of course, I would be lying. To be honest, they're a bit dull. But making a design specification is a vital step in
designing and manufacturing a new product. So learn about it.

# Generating Proposals

Now hold on to your hats, my wild young things — this is where it all starts to get a bit more <u>interesting</u>.
This is the <u>creative</u> bit. This is where you start <u>generating ideas</u>.

## There are a few Tricks that can help you Get Started

The following are suggestions to help you get started with designing:

1) Create a <u>mood board</u> — this is a load of different images, words, materials, colours and so on that might trigger ideas for your design.

2) <u>Brainstorm</u> — think up key words, questions and initial thoughts relating to your product. Start off by just writing whatever ideas come into your head and analyse them later — see p26.

3) Work from an <u>existing product</u> — but change some of its features or production methods so that it fits in with your <u>specification</u>.

4) Break the task up into smaller parts — design the 'look' of the product (<u>aesthetics</u>), then look at the <u>technology</u> involved and so on.

## You need to Come up with a Range of Designs

1) You need to <u>annotate</u> (i.e. add <u>notes</u> to) your designs to fully <u>explain</u> your ideas. These notes could be about:

> - materials
> - sizes
> - user
> - shape
> - cost
> - advantages and disadvantages
> - production method
> - functions

2) You need to produce a <u>wide range</u> of <u>appropriate</u> solutions that you think could <u>actually be made</u>.

3) Try to use a <u>range of techniques</u> for presenting your designs. A good thing to do is to use different drawing techniques — for example:

> - perspective
> - orthographic projection
> - cross-sections
> - freehand sketching
> - digital camera photos
> - isometric projection

**Design Proposal for Winter Bikini**

Wide straps

Fake-fur fabric

High waist to aid belly warmth

Elasticated waist and legs for a snug fit.

<u>Advantages:</u>
Allows bikini-lovers to wear bikinis in cold weather.

<u>Disadvantages:</u>
Fake-fur fabric might be difficult to wash. Might be difficult to swim in.

4) Once you've got a few possible designs, you need to <u>check</u> that each one <u>matches</u> your <u>specification</u> — any that don't will <u>not</u> be <u>suitable</u>.

5) Finally, you need to choose <u>one</u> of your suitable designs to <u>develop further</u>.

## <u>Write whatever comes to mind — no hope for me then...</u>

Think what someone will need to know to fully appreciate your design, and include this information on your proposal. And remember — you need to do quite a few of these so that you can choose the best one to develop and improve. This is the bit where you need to get your creative head on.

# Development

Once you've decided on a design, you can begin to <u>develop</u> it further.
This is when your design should start to really <u>take shape</u>.

## You can Develop your Design in Different Ways

Depending on the <u>type</u> of product that's being produced, further development might involve:

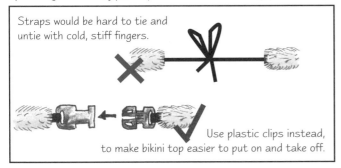

Straps would be hard to tie and untie with cold, stiff fingers.

Use plastic clips instead, to make bikini top easier to put on and take off.

1) producing further <u>sketches</u> — but in more detail.

2) <u>modelling</u> and <u>testing</u> your idea. Or <u>experimenting</u> with different aspects of the design.
E.g. you could try various materials, sizes and production methods.

3) using <u>people's opinions</u> about what you've done to help you arrive at a satisfactory solution.

## Modelling means Trying Things Out

It can be useful to make a <u>prototype</u> or <u>model</u> of your idea, especially if it's difficult to draw.

1) Try out <u>different aspects</u> of your design. If your design is quite complicated, it may help to break it down into smaller, more manageable parts and test them individually.

2) Use a digital camera to <u>record</u> your models.

3) <u>Evaluate</u> the models (see next page), <u>identifying reasons</u> for selecting or rejecting different designs.

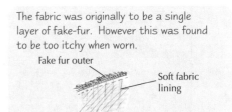

The fabric was originally to be a single layer of fake-fur. However this was found to be too itchy when worn.

Fake fur outer

Soft fabric lining

This was remedied by adding a lining.

> This is a vital part of the design process. Ideally you should <u>solve all the potential problems</u> with your design at this stage.

## Use the Results to Make Modifications

1) Results from your modelling and from your evaluation (see next page) will help you make important <u>modifications</u> (changes) to improve the product, and help it meet the design <u>specification</u>.

2) Suggested improvements could be:
   • ways to make the <u>product itself better</u>,
   • suggestions to make it more suitable for <u>batch or mass production</u>.

3) But make sure you keep a <u>record</u> of whatever it is you find out (see next page).

4) Once you've made a modification to your design, you'll need to <u>try it out</u> to see if it actually improves things.

5) You might find that you end up modifying something, then trying it out, then making another modification and trying that out, then making another modification and trying that out, and so on. That's <u>just the way it goes</u> sometimes. Make sure you record ALL the changes you make and why.

## Modification — wear a parka and ride a scooter...

Modelling and evaluation *(see next page)* go hand in hand. It's pointless making a piece of clothing and trying it on if you're not going to bother learning anything from it. ...Unless you didn't have any clothes.

# Evaluation

Evaluation is an important part of any product development process,
and needs to be done at various stages along the way.

## Keep Records of your Research and Testing

1) As you develop your product, keep records of any testing or market research you do.
   Write it all down, keep it, and refer back to it.

2) You might have tested materials for suitability, or tested components to see how well they work —
   but whatever you did, you need to write down all the results.

3) Compare the good and bad points of existing products with your model or prototype.
   Ask yourself if your product does the job better. Record your results.

4) Find out people's opinions and preferences about your models and prototypes (see previous page).
   This will help you to refine your ideas so you can arrive at the best solution.

5) Questionnaires help here — relevant market research questions might include:

> - Does the product work well?
> - Does the product work as well as similar products on the market?
> - Does the product look good? Is it well styled and modern-looking?
> - Are you unsure about any of the features? If so, which ones and why?
> - If this product were on the market, would you consider buying it?
> - If you were buying it, which price range do you think it would fall into?
> - Do you prefer another similar product to this one?

This type of evaluation is called formative evaluation —
it's being used to help form the final design.

*Product testing in Greenland*

## Now You should Know Exactly what You're Making

By the time you've finished developing your ideas and have arrived at a final design, you should
have found out / worked out:

1) The best materials, tools and other equipment to use (and their availability).

2) The approximate manufacturing time needed to make each item.

3) How much it should cost to manufacture each item.

4) The most appropriate assembly process — this is going to be important information when it comes to
   planning production, and can be in the form of a flow chart (see page 8).

## If you don't know what you're doing now, you never will...

At this stage of the process it should be crystal clear in your own mind how your final product should look, and
how you're going to make it. But you're not finished yet. No, no, no, no, no... There's still the little business of
actually making your pride and joy. Oh what fun... what fun...

# Manufacturer's Specification

Now that you know <u>exactly</u> what you're going to make, you need to <u>communicate</u> all that info to the person that's actually going to <u>make</u> it.

## You need to produce a Manufacturer's Specification

A manufacturer's specification can be a written <u>series of statements</u>, or <u>working drawings</u> and <u>sequence diagrams</u>. It has to explain <u>exactly</u> how the product will be made, and should include:

1) Clear <u>construction</u> details explaining <u>exactly</u> how each bit's going to be made.

2) The <u>materials</u> and <u>components</u> to be used, and any special <u>finishes</u>.

3) <u>Sizes</u> — <u>precise measurements</u> of each part.

4) <u>Tolerances</u> — the maximum and minimum sizes each part should be.

5) <u>Quality Control</u> instructions — where, when and how the manufacturing process should be checked. (See page 8 for time planning and page 27 for quality control.)

6) <u>Costings</u> — how much each part costs and details of any other costs involved.

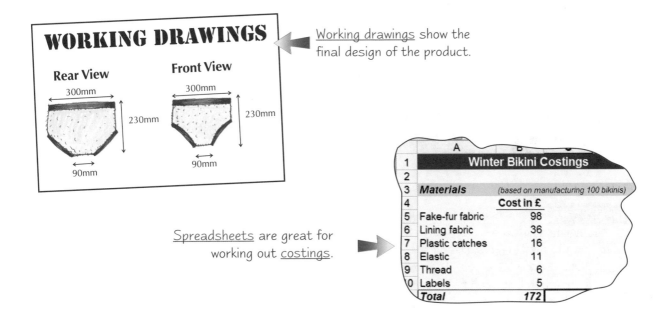

<u>Working drawings</u> show the final design of the product.

<u>Spreadsheets</u> are great for working out <u>costings</u>.

## Plan how long the Production Process should take

When you get to this stage of product development, you also need to plan:

1) how your methods might have to <u>change</u> now you're producing the product <u>in volume</u>.

2) <u>each stage</u> of the process in a great deal of <u>detail</u>.

3) <u>how long</u> each stage will take.

4) what needs to be <u>prepared</u> before you can start each stage.

5) how you will <u>ensure consistency</u> and <u>quality</u>.

See the <u>next page</u> as well for some different ways to help with this planning.

## Manufacturer's specification — fur, fur and more fur...

You know what they say... the devil's in the detail. Yeah, well, I don't know exactly what that means, but it's probably got something to do with being really precise. And that's what you've got to do with your manufacturer's specification, or your masterpiece could end up as a dog's dinner.

# Planning Production

Making one or two examples of your product is (relatively) easy.
But mass-producing it is a whole different ball game — and it takes a shed-load of careful planning.

## Use Charts to help you

You need to work out how long each stage will take, and how these times will fit into the total time you've allowed for production. There are different ways of doing this:

(1) **Work Order** — This can be produced as a table or flow chart. The purpose of a work order is to plan in sequence each task to be carried out. This will also include: tools and equipment, quality control stages, safety, and so on.

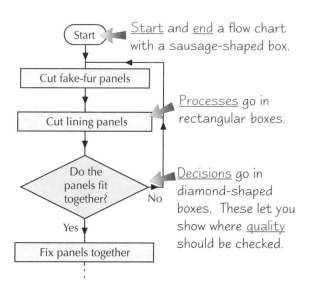

Start and end a flow chart with a sausage-shaped box.

Processes go in rectangular boxes.

Decisions go in diamond-shaped boxes. These let you show where quality should be checked.

(2) **Gantt Chart** — This is a time plan showing the management of tasks. The tasks are listed down the left-hand side, and the timing plotted across the top. The coloured squares show how long each task takes, and the order they're done in.

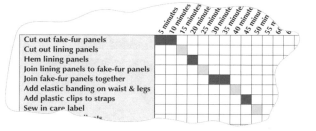

## Test that the Product Works and Meets the Specification

1) When you think you've got the final product, it's vital to test it. Most important of all, you have to make sure it works, and meets the original design specification.

2) More questionnaires or surveys may help here. Ask a wide range of people to give their opinions about the finished product.

3) If your product fails to match any part of the specification, you must explain why. You really have to stand back and have a good hard think about your work. If you aren't satisfied with the way any part of the process went, think of how you could put it right for next time.
Write it down in the form of a report.

4) This type of final evaluation is called summative evaluation — it summarises what you've learnt.

## There's nothing like a good chart...

That's all you have to do then when it comes to your project. Just do in a few short weeks pretty much what it takes people in industry several months to complete, and you've got no worries.

# Revision Summary

*So that's the section over with, and what a roller-coaster ride full of fun and excitement it was. Yeah, well the fun's not over yet, so don't look so disappointed. There's still some exciting revision questions for you to tackle. So try the questions, and then have a look back through the section to see if you got them all right. If you did — great. But if you got any wrong, have another careful read of the section and then <u>try the questions again</u>. And keep doing this until you can get all the questions right. That way, you know you're learning stuff.*

1) What is the name given to the whole process of designing and making something?

2) Give three reasons why a new product might be needed.

3) Describe the kind of information you should put in your design brief.

4) Give three ways in which research can help you when you're designing a new product.

5) Explain how a questionnaire can be useful.

6) Give two methods other than a questionnaire that you could use to carry out research.

7) What is the name given to the process of drawing conclusions from your research?

8) Explain what is meant by a design specification.

9) Why might some points in a design specification be hard to assess just by looking at the product?

10) When would you compile an initial design specification?

11) Give three ways of getting started on your design ideas.

12) What does the word 'annotate' mean?

13) What information should you include in your designs?

14) Why should you aim to produce a number of design ideas?

15) Give three techniques for presenting your designs.

16) Name two ways of developing your designs further.

17) Explain why it's useful to model your designs.

18) Describe two kinds of improvement you could make to your design.

19) When should you make an evaluation of your design?
a) at the end of the project   b) throughout the project   c) evaluation is for wimps and sissies.

20) What is meant by the phrase 'formative evaluation'?
Describe two ways of evaluating your work in this way.

21) Explain why a manufacturer's specification needs to be very precise.

22) Give four kinds of information that need to be on a manufacturer's specification.

23) When using a Gantt chart, what information goes down the left-hand side?

24) Describe two methods of planning how long the manufacturing process should take.

25) Describe the process of 'summative evaluation'.

# Fibres and Fabrics

Most <u>fabrics</u> are constructed from <u>yarns</u>. And most <u>yarns</u> are made from <u>fibres</u>.

## Fibres are the Tiny Bits that make up Yarns

Fibres are <u>fine</u>, <u>hair-like</u> structures. They are available in either fixed lengths (called <u>staple lengths</u>) or long, <u>continuous filaments</u>. They come from three main sources:

1) <u>NATURAL FIBRES</u> come from natural sources such as plants and animals (e.g. cotton comes from plants, wool comes from sheep and other animals). They are cut into staple lengths.

2) <u>REGENERATED FIBRES</u> come from natural sources which are then treated with chemicals to make fibres.

3) <u>SYNTHETIC FIBRES</u> are man-made. They're made from chemicals (which come mainly from coal or oil).

Both regenerated and synthetic fibres are made into <u>filaments</u>. They can be <u>cut</u> to produce staple lengths.

## Yarn — the proper word for a Thread

<u>Natural fibres</u> are first <u>harvested</u>, then <u>cleaned</u>, then <u>straightened</u>, then last (but not least) <u>spun</u> into yarn.

<u>Regenerated</u> or <u>synthetic</u> fibres are made in one of three ways.
The way chosen depends on the polymer (substance) used.

1) <u>Wet spinning</u> — a polymer solution is pushed through tiny holes into a chemical bath to form filaments. The chemicals cause the fibres to harden.

2) <u>Dry spinning</u> — a polymer solution is pushed through tiny holes into a stream of warm air. The warm air causes the fibres to harden.

3) <u>Melt spinning</u> — the polymer is melted, then pushed through tiny holes, then cooled to form filaments.

The resulting <u>filaments</u> are then <u>spun</u> to produce <u>yarns</u>.

## Fabrics — made of Yarns which are Woven, Knitted or Bonded

Fabrics are made of yarns which are either <u>woven</u>, <u>knitted</u> or <u>bonded</u> together.

### 1) <u>Woven fabrics</u>

have <u>two</u> yarns, the <u>warp</u> and the <u>weft</u>. The warp travels up and down the weave, the weft from right to left.

<u>Plain weave</u> is the simplest weave. The weft thread passes over and under alternate warp threads.

<u>Satin weave</u> is when the weft thread goes under several warp threads and over one. There are more threads lying on the surface so the fabric looks shiny.

*<u>Twill weave</u> creates a diagonal pattern on the surface of the fabric. Used to make strong, close weaves such as denim.*

### 2) <u>Knitted Construction</u>

Knitted fabrics have a <u>looped structure</u> and <u>stretch</u> more than woven fabrics. There are various types.

<u>Weft Knitting</u> — yarn runs across the fabric making loops with the row of yarn beneath. Can be produced by hand or machine. e.g. single jersey, ribknit and double jersey.

<u>Warp knitting</u> — the yarn runs "up" the fabric, rather like the warp yarns of woven fabric. Can only be made by machine.

### 3) <u>Non-woven Fabrics</u>

<u>Bonded fabrics</u> are made with "webs" of fabric held together by glue, needle-punching or stitch bonding. e.g. interlinings, liners for floppy discs and artificial leathers.

<u>Felting</u> is an older way of making non-woven fabric. It is made by combining moisture, heat and pressure. Felt is used for many things including carpet underlay, craft material and hats.

## <u>Aren't fabwics twilling — We'd be beweft without them...</u>

It's easy to know warp from weft, 'cos weft goes from weft to right (teehee). The rest needs some careful learning, as there's lots of detail, and some nasty technical bits. You'll soon be able to spot a twill weave at 50 metres...

# Fabrics — Properties and Characteristics

Ahhh... just what you wanted — a page all about <u>fabrics</u>. You've got to know them <u>all</u>.

| NAME | ORIGIN | DESCRIPTION | STRENGTH | ABSORBENCY | FLAME RESISTANCE | USES |
|---|---|---|---|---|---|---|
| COTTON | Ripened seed pods of the cotton plant. | Strong, absorbent, easy to care for, cheap, creases easily. | *** | **** | * | Denim, calico, chintz, lawn, drill. Jeans, T-shirts, blouses, soft furnishings. |
| LINEN | Stalks of the flax plant. | Very strong, absorbent, cheap (though the price is rising). | *** | **** | * | Lawn, batiste. Trousers, suits, dresses, furnishings. |
| SILK | From the cocoon of the silk moth. | Silky, smooth, soft, drapes well, expensive. | **** | **** | **** | Chiffon, crepe, organza, velvet. Lingerie, underwear, dresses, shirts, ties. |
| WOOL | Fleece of the sheep. | Warm, soft, absorbent, crease resistant, fairly expensive. | ** | **** | **** | Felt, gabardine, knitted fabrics. Suits, dresses, carpet. |
| VISCOSE | Regenerated fibre made from wood pulp treated with chemicals. | Absorbent, drapes well, smooth, light. | ** | **** | * | Lingerie, underwear, dresses, suits, skirts, linings, soft furnishings. Regenerated fibres are very versatile. They can be used for almost anything. |
| ACETATE | Regenerated fibre made from wood pulp treated with acetic acid. | Soft, smooth, resistant to sunlight, mildew. | ** | *** | * | |

Natural Fibres (Cotton, Linen, Silk, Wool). Regenerated Fibres (Viscose, Acetate).

## *I love the feel of moth larvae excretions against my naked skin....*

Make sure you learn all this fascinating stuff about where different fabrics come from and what they're used for. Your lingerie may not seem quite as glam once you know that it's made from chemically treated wood pulp — but at least that explains why it burns so well. No more semi-naked fire walking for me... not after reading this page.

# More Fabrics — Properties and Characteristics

Ahhh... just what you wanted — another page all about <u>fabrics</u>. You've got to know these synthetic ones too.

| NAME | ORIGIN | DESCRIPTION | STRENGTH | ABSORBENCY | FLAME RESISTANCE | USES |
|---|---|---|---|---|---|---|
| POLYESTER | Chemically produced from oil. | Strong, smooth, elastic, crease resistant. | **** | * | ** | Sportswear. Often combined with other fibres such as cotton. |
| NYLON | Chemically produced from two different substances. | Strong, warm, elastic, crease resistant. | **** | * | ** | Sportswear, furnishings, carpets, tights and socks. |
| TACTEL | Derived from Nylon. | Highest strength to weight ratio of any fibre. | ***** | * | ** | Skiwear and lingerie. |
| ACRYLIC | Chemically produced from oil. | Soft, warm, similar to wool. | ** | * | * | Fake fur, knitted clothing, furnishings. |
| ELASTANE (LYCRA) | A type of polyurethane. | Extremely elastic. Can stretch 7 times its length. Keeps its shape well. | *** | * | * | Often combined with other fibres. Sportswear, fashion clothing, underwear. |
| ARAMID (KEVLAR) | Chemically produced. | Extremely strong (4 times stronger than steel wire). Highly flame retardant. | ****** | * | **** | Bullet proof vests, cables, conveyor belts, high performance tyres. |

Synthetic Fibres

## _Imagine a world without lycra — lovely baggy swimming costumes..._

Where would we be without modern artificial fabrics? Well we wouldn't spend as much time freezing our bums off up mountains, swimming, water-skiing or being shot — we wouldn't have the technical clothing to do it in. More nasty little details to learn here I'm afraid. KNOW YOUR FABRICS...

# Fabric Blends and Mixtures

Many fabrics are made from a blend or mix of different fibres.

## Blends are Different Fibres made into a Single Yarn

1) A blend is when two or more different fibres are used to produce a single yarn.

2) These fibres are blended before or during spinning.

3) Polyester cotton is a popular blend.

## Mixtures are Fabrics made of Different Yarns

A mix is when a fabric is made up of two or more different fibres —
one fibre for the warp yarn and another for the weft yarn.

## What's the Point of Mixtures and Blends?

1) One fibre by itself may not give you exactly what you want.
Combining different fibres often gives you the best characteristics of both.

**EXAMPLE**

| Cotton | Polyester |
|--------|-----------|
| Absorbent and soft | Not very absorbent or soft |
| Takes a long time to dry | Dries quickly |
| Creases easily and hard to iron | Doesn't crease much so needs little ironing |

By combining polyester and cotton you get an easy care fabric that:
• *IS SOFT AND COMFORTABLE,* • *DRIES QUICKLY,* • *IS EASY TO IRON.*

2) Combining fibres sometimes reduces costs.
For example, combining a cheap fibre with a more expensive one often gives you
many of the characteristics of the expensive one but makes the fabric cheaper.

3) You can also get different textures and colours by combining different fibres.
You can create interesting textures by combining fibres of different textures.
Some fibres absorb dyes more easily than others. Combining different fibres which
are then dyed can create interesting colour effects. This is known as cross-dyeing.

## Mixing and Blending Fibres can affect the Safety of Fabrics

**EXAMPLE — Flammability**

*Cotton is highly flammable. Polyester has low flammability.*

1) Combining cotton with polyester would create a fabric that is highly flammable.

2) If polyester fabric is stitched with cotton sewing thread the flame will run along the stitching.

3) Safety regulations insist that thermoplastic (e.g. polyester) thread is used on nightclothes
to reduce the fire risk.

## A blend? I like my clothing to be single malt, if you don't mind...

Is your wool not stretchy enough? Is your lycra too thin and shiny? Then try 'Stretchy-Wool' our new lycra-wool
blend — it's stretchy and woolly. Ideal for winter swimming. The stylish alternative to the fur-bikini...
Make sure you understand the difference between a mixture and a blend — and then learn the rest of the page too.

# Modern and Smart Fabrics

Hi-tech fabrics have been developed over recent years, which means designers can make new exciting products.

## New fibres have been developed from Natural Sources

1) New fibres have been developed from natural sources,
e.g. pineapple fibre, banana fibre, ramie (made from a shrub).

2) Salmon skin is now used as an alternative to leather.

3) Natural fibres are usually environmentally friendly and biodegradable.

## New Fibres and Fabrics are Constantly being Developed

1) Lycra was introduced in the UK in the 1950s. It's strong, lightweight and very stretchy. Lycra is now used in a wide variety of clothing such as jeans, swimwear, leggings, evening wear.

2) Teflon is well-known for making nonstick pans, but now it can be made into fabrics. It's used in waterproof clothing and surgical gowns.

3) Tencel is a fabric that has been recently developed. It feels like silk but breathes like cotton. It's machine-washable and easy to dye. It's also environmentally friendly because it's made from wood pulp from sustainable forests.

4) Gore-Tex is a breathable fabric. Gore-Tex allows perspiration to rise to the outer layer along a chain of hydrophilic (water-attracting) molecules. But the rain just bounces off, keeping you dry.

## Microfibres are Tiny — Finer even than Silk

1) Microfibres are usually made from polyester (a man-made fibre).

2) They can be blended with cotton.

3) Microfibres can be woven or knitted.

4) They can be woven so closely that they prevent water penetrating the fabric but also allow perspiration to escape. They are great for waterproof clothing that keeps you dry.

5) Microfibre fabric is soft, comfortable to wear, lightweight, lasts well and hangs beautifully. It's often blended with natural fibres like cotton, linen or silk to reduce costs.

## Smart Fabrics change their Properties and Characteristics

1) Smart fabrics can change their properties and characteristics depending on their environment.

2) Some fabrics are printed with special printing inks that change colour according to the temperature.

3) Some fabrics change colour when you see them at different angles. The fabric is covered with a fine plastic layer of tiny lenses that refract light.

4) Fragrances can now be added to fabric to make them always smell good.

## My T-shirt goes brown under the armpits when I sweat — lovely...

Plenty to learn on this page. Some of these fabrics are already really important, like Gore-Tex, which is now used in lots of outdoor clothing. Smart materials aren't used much yet but could become really important in the future. Basically, you just need to be aware of all the cool developments in the clothes world...

# Fabric Combinations

Like the <u>sweetness</u> of chocolate? Love <u>lumpy</u> gravy? Why not eat chocolate gravy — it's sweet *and* lumpy. OK, maybe a (very, very) bad idea — but combining <u>two fabrics</u> is often a <u>good</u> idea.

## Combine Two Fabrics to Get the Good Qualities of Both

Two or more fabrics can be <u>combined</u> to give you the <u>best qualities</u> from each one. For example, a <u>waterproof</u> fabric can be stitched to a lining made of a <u>warmer</u> fabric to make a garment that's warm *and* waterproof.

## Interfacing Makes Fabric Firmer

Interfacing is a <u>stiff</u> fabric available in strips.
It can be <u>combined</u> with most fabrics to give <u>strength</u> and <u>stiffness</u>.
Interfacing can be <u>ironed on</u> or <u>sewn on</u>.

## Fabrics can be Quilted in Layers to Give Warmth

Different fabrics can be quilted together in layers (see page 18) to provide warmth.

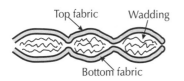

Top fabric   Wadding

Bottom fabric

Examples of quilted textile products are anoraks, body warmers and bed quilts.

## Fabrics Can be Combined by Laminating or Coating

### LAMINATING

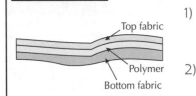

Top fabric

Polymer
Bottom fabric

1) Laminating is when two or more layers of fabric are combined with a middle layer of <u>polymer</u> (a type of compound) which sticks to both surfaces.

2) Laminated fabrics can use a <u>delicate</u> lace or knitted fabric together with a <u>stronger</u> woven fabric to provide <u>strength</u> and <u>firmness</u>.

### COATING

1) Coating is when a layer of <u>polymer film</u> is applied to the <u>surface</u> of the fabric.

2) Coated fabrics are often used for <u>waterproof</u> but "<u>breathable</u>" fabrics. They work by conducting perspiration to the outer surface of the fabric along a chain of hydrophilic (water attracting) molecules.

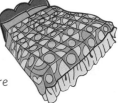

3) <u>PVC coatings</u> are often given to cotton or viscose to make <u>protective garments</u> in industry.

4) Examples of laminated and coated fabrics include: tents, ski-wear, sportswear, survival suits and surgical clothing.

## *I gave my dog a PVC coating — he's now rainproof and wipe-clean...*

Make sure you've got the differences between mixing, blending and combining fibres and fabric clear in your head. They're all done so that the properties of different materials can be combined, but they are three very different methods of doing this. Don't neglect interfacing and quilting either — where would you be without a good duvet...

# Dyeing Fabric

You can change the colour of fabric to make it more interesting. There are various ways of doing this.

## There are Natural Dyes and Chemical Dyes

1)  Until the 1850s all dyes were <u>natural</u>. Natural dyes can be made from onions, beetroot, tea, raspberries etc.
2)  <u>Chemical dyes</u> were invented in the 1850s. The <u>advantages</u> of chemical dyes are that:

    a) *The colours are brighter and clearer.*    c) *They're easier to make.*
    b) *They're cheaper to make.*    d) *The same colour can be achieved repeatedly.*

## Some Fabrics are Better for Dyeing than Others

1)  <u>Natural</u> fibres are the <u>best</u> for dyeing as they're very <u>absorbent</u>. Examples are cotton, linen, wool and silk.
2)  The <u>colour of the fabric</u> you begin with makes a difference to the final colour.

    *For example — if you dye white fabric red, you get red fabric. If you dye yellow fabric red, you get orange.*

### Tie and Dye is one of the oldest methods of dyeing fabric

1)  Fabric is <u>tied</u> with string or rubber bands.
2)  The fabric is then immersed in dye.
3)  The tied areas <u>don't absorb</u> the dye and this is how the pattern is made.

*There are various ways to tie the fabric before dyeing. Here are some examples:*

Elastic bands or ties →

### Batik — Uses Areas of Wax to Stop the Dye Being Absorbed

1)  <u>Hot wax</u> is applied with a brush or tjanting tool (a pointed tool used for dripping the wax).
2)  The wax is allowed to <u>dry</u>.
3)  The <u>dye</u> is applied.
4)  The wax is <u>ironed off</u> to reveal the pattern.

### Silk Painting Can Be Used for Detailed Designs

<u>Silk painting</u> uses a liquid called <u>gutta</u>. This stops the dye penetrating areas of the fabric.

1)  The gutta is applied to the silk. It is allowed to dry.
2)  The dye is applied with a brush.
3)  The dye is <u>fixed</u> with <u>heat</u> (ironed or steamed).

*Tie dye, Batik and Silk Painting using gutta are all resist techniques.*

## Stencilling is Really Good for Repeat Patterns

1)  <u>Stencilling</u> is when shapes are <u>cut</u> from paper, card or acetate sheets.

2)  <u>Paint</u> is then applied <u>through</u> the <u>cut-outs</u> with a sponge or brush.

3)  Stencils enable you to <u>repeat</u> a design again and again.

<u>*Use of ICT*</u>
*\* You can create designs for stencils using a graphics or CAD program.*
*\* Your designs can be printed directly onto card or acetate.*

## You Can Colour Fabric with Special Paint and Pens

*These are sometimes called a "<u>direct application method</u>".*

<u>Fabric paints</u> are applied with a <u>brush</u> or <u>sponge</u>.
<u>Fabric crayons</u> can be used to give <u>bold lines</u> or <u>textured effects</u> with or without <u>stencils</u>.
<u>Fabric pens</u> are very good for adding <u>detail</u> and <u>fine lines</u>.

## <u>Shocking statistic no.92 — 0.016% of people dye on the toilet...</u>

Learn all these fun things you can do to fabric in the comfort of your own home (doing it on the loo is not recommended).

# Fabric Printing

There are three main methods of fabric printing: <u>block printing</u>, <u>roller printing</u> and <u>screen printing</u>.

## *Block Printing has Been Around a Long Time*

1) *A design is drawn on a <u>block</u> and then the background is cut away, leaving the design <u>raised</u>.*
2) *<u>Printing ink</u> is then applied to the <u>raised surface</u> of the block.*
3) *The block is then <u>pressed down</u> onto the fabric.*

People have been block printing for <u>over 2000 years</u>.

Block printing has <u>disadvantages</u> :
- it's <u>time consuming</u>,
- it's not good for <u>fine detail</u>,
- a <u>different block</u> is needed for each colour.

## *Roller Printing is Quick*

1) <u>Roller printing</u> was invented by a Scotsman called Bell.
2) The design is put onto <u>rollers</u> which are inked as the fabric is <u>continuously run</u> under them.
2) This method made the printing of fabric much <u>quicker</u>. <u>Different colours</u> can be printed at the <u>same time</u>. Roller printing is a <u>cheap</u> printing method.
3) However, there are some disadvantages.
- The rollers are <u>expensive</u>.
- The <u>size</u> of the pattern depends on the size of the roller.
- <u>Blotches</u> can happen when you are printing <u>large areas</u>.

## *There are Two Methods of Screen Printing: Rotary and Flat-bed*

### FLAT-BED SCREEN PRINTING

<u>Screen printing</u> was developed from stencilling. It was used a lot in Japan.
<u>Intricate</u> designs can be printed well. It's good for printing <u>large areas</u> of colour.

*Method*:

1) *A stencil is cut from card or acetate, either by hand or by using CAD/CAM.*
2) *A screen covered with fine mesh is used. The stencil is laid beneath.*
3) *Printing ink is poured onto the screen.*
4) *A squeegee is pressed down and drawn firmly across the screen, forcing the printing ink through the mesh.*
6) *The screen is lifted up and the design is left.*

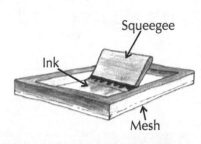

Squeegee

Ink

Mesh

- In industry the squeegee is replaced by metal rods that move backwards and forwards across the screen.
- Several screens can be used one after the other to produce complicated designs of many colours.

### ROTARY SCREEN PRINTING

1) This is the <u>fastest</u> and <u>most used</u> method of printing fabric. 300m of fabric can be printed every minute.
2) A different coloured dye is pumped into each of a series of cylinders. The dye is forced through a <u>fine wire mesh</u> onto fabric that passes below.

## *Block, roller and screen — three ways to print, three things to learn...*

Printing — what a fascinating subject. It's about as exciting as watching ink dry. Anyway, just learn how to do it and then you can move on and learn about something even more exciting, like how buttons work...

# Fabric Decoration

A textile product can be made more interesting by "embellishment" (decoration).

## Appliqué is Sewing Bits of Fabric On Top

1) Appliqué is a very old technique.

2) The oldest piece of appliqué found was dated at 980 BC (i.e. 3000 years old).

3) Cultures all over the world use appliqué, including India, Pakistan, Russia, Central and South America.

4) Appliqué involves placing one fabric onto another and sewing them together. A close zig-zag stitch is usually used — different stitches and coloured thread can be used for added decorative effect.

5) Beads, sequins or intricate embroidery can be worked over the top for further effect.

## Padded Appliqué is Appliqué with... Padding

1) Appliqué can be padded by placing wadding or stuffing between the fabric pieces.

2) This creates a 3D effect and gives depth.

## Quilting Can Give a Decorative Effect

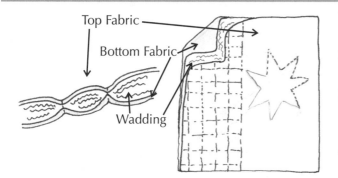

1) Like padded appliqué, quilting also involves placing wadding between two layers of fabric.

2) The fabrics are then stitched together in straight lines or in a pattern.

3) Quilting is often used to give added warmth to a product (e.g. an anorak or bed quilt). The wadding traps warm air between the layers of fabric.

4) Quilting can give a 3D effect.

## Embroidery is Decorative Stitching

1) Embroidery is decorative stitching.

2) Very intricate details can be achieved by hand or by machine.

3) Industrial embroidery machines are often used to produce logos, motifs and badges as well as embroidery.

**Examples of Embroidery Stitches**

Chain stitch    Herringbone stitch    Blanket stitch

## The Dark Art of Embroidery — the preserve of haggard old crones...

I really like embroidery — it takes up all those useless hours I would otherwise have frittered away hang-gliding, or learning to speak German. My blanket stitch is so neat now that it makes old ladies weep, and my cross stitch is a real winner with the lads. But you know something's wrong when you start embellishing your embellishments...

# Fabric Finishes

Fabric finishes (sometimes called performance finishes) can be given to fabrics to improve them in some way.

## Finishes Make a Fabric More Suitable for Its Purpose

There are four basic reasons why finishes are given:

1) To modify (change) the surface (e.g. smoothing, embossing, raising).
2) To modify wearing properties (e.g. crease resistance, stain resistance).
3) To modify aftercare characteristics (e.g. shrinking).
4) To modify the appearance (e.g. bleaching).

Finishes are usually the last stage of fabric processing.

## A Stain Resistant Finish Keeps Your Fabric Clean

1) To give stain resistance, a fabric can be finished with a mixture of silicone and fluorine.
2) This stops grease and dirt penetrating the fabric.
3) It is used a lot for carpets and upholstery.

## Don't Go Up in Flames — Add Flame Retardant

1) Flame retardant finishes improve the flammability performance of a fabric (i.e. make it less likely to catch fire).
2) Some finishes do this by making the fabric unable to give off flammable fuel vapours.
3) Some finishes make vapours that suppress fire. The most widely used are "Durovatex" and "Proban".
4) These finishes are carefully designed so they don't spoil the feel, strength or wear of the fabric.

## A Crease Resistant Finish Means Fabric Creases Less

1) Some fabrics (such as cotton, linen and rayon) crease easily.
2) Finishes can be given to these fabrics to improve their crease resistance.
3) These finishes are thermoplastic (synthetic plastic) so they become soft and pliable at high temperatures. Therefore finishes can also be heat-set into shape (e.g. pleats or trouser creases can be made permanent).

## Brush Your Fabric To Give A Soft, Raised Surface

1) Fabrics can be brushed by passing them through a large revolving brush. This raises the surface of the fabric.
2) The raised surface traps air and keeps the body warmer.
3) Baby clothes are often brushed for this reason.

## Some Finishes are Really Smart

Smart finishes are just that little bit clever...

1) For example some finishes make the fabric change colour.
2) Others are given to fabric so that it smells really nice (all the time).
3) Some are antibacterial (i.e. they zap nasty germs).
4) Others respond to changes in light, heat or pressure.

## With super powers like these I could... take over the world

He was born out of tragedy, the result of a freak accident at a textiles factory. He cannot stain, he cannot burn, he cannot be ironed flat... Now follow the exciting adventures of Clean Inflammable Permanently Creased Boy...

# Fabric Care

Textile products are made from a wide range of fibres and fabrics which need to be cared for in different ways.

## There is a Standard Code for Fabric Care Symbols

An <u>International Textile Care Labelling Code</u> (ITCLC) has been developed with <u>symbols</u> to tell people <u>how to care</u> for their textile products. <u>Washing machines</u> have these symbols on their washing programs. The care symbols are also on <u>garment labels</u> and packets of <u>washing powder</u>.

## Care Labels Tell You How to Care for a Garment

A <u>care label</u> is a fabric label stitched permanently into a garment.
A good care label contains the following information:

1) <u>Fibre content</u> (this is compulsory)

2) Any special <u>finishes</u> or <u>treatments</u>

3) <u>Cleaning</u> instructions

4) <u>Size</u> of the garment

100% PURE SILK
HAND OR MACHINE
WASH SEPARATELY
EXTRA LARGE

## Learn the Most Common Textile Care Code Symbols

Here are the most <u>frequently used</u> symbols from the <u>Textiles Care Code</u>:

| WASHING | |
|---|---|
| [40°] | Maximum temperature 40° |
| [60°] | Maximum temperature 60° |
| (hand) | Hand wash only |
| ⊠ | Do not bleach |

| IRONING | |
|---|---|
| (iron •) | Cool iron |
| (iron ••) | Warm iron |
| (iron •••) | Hot iron |
| ⊠ | Do not iron |

| DRYING | |
|---|---|
| ◯ | Tumble dry beneficial |
| ⊠ | Do not tumble dry |

| DRY CLEANING | |
|---|---|
| Ⓐ | Dry clean in all solvents |
| ⊗ | Do not dry clean |

## Information Labelling Gives Extra Information On A Product

Information labels give <u>extra information</u> about a product that the manufacturer wants to tell you (e.g. a <u>logo</u>, the <u>make</u> or <u>special fabric</u> information). These labels are <u>temporarily attached</u> to a garment and are often made of <u>card</u> or <u>plastic</u>.

PURE NEW WOOL

## The Goods You Buy Must be Fit for Purpose

1) <u>Consumer legislation</u> says that textile goods <u>must</u> be "<u>fit for purpose</u>".
   This means that the product you buy must be <u>suitable</u> for the purpose it was designed for.

2) For example, if you buy bed sheets that need to be <u>washed frequently</u>,
   then the manufacturer <u>must make sure</u> that they <u>can</u> be washed and will wear reasonably well.

3) If the label on your bed sheets says that they can be washed at 60°, then this <u>must</u> be true.

## I found this under my armpit: (hand) ⊠

Real lessons for life here. When you leave home and you have to do all your own washing you'll be glad that you read this page properly. Shrinking your £50 pure lamb's wool sweater to the size of a beer mat is no laughing matter.

# Components

Components are bits of things used in addition to the main fabric, e.g. thread, buttons, zips.
They may be functional, decorative or both.

## Components are Pre-manufactured Parts

1) Components are often needed to complete your design and make task.

2) They usually have a practical purpose, such as closing a garment, but sometimes they can be purely decorative, like a lace edging.

- Without components your product might be dull or useless.
  - Components can be used to provide closure.
- They can improve the shape and hang of a garment.
  - They can be used just for fun as design accents.

## Choose the Right Components

The components you choose should:

- lay flat
- be the correct size and weight for your fabric
- be firmly secured
- be suitable for the purpose

You really need to know what's on offer, so you'll be able to create more exciting designs.

1) Thread — used for joining, top stitching and embroidery. Select the correct thread for the job.

2) Fastenings — buttons, zips, Velcro, press studs, hooks and eyes, ribbons, laces & toggles.

3) Decorative Components — lace, marabou, fringing, beads, sequins, braid, pre-manufactured collars and cuffs, electronic noise and movement components.

4) Structural Components, to give shape — boning, shoulder pads, bondaweb, elastic & bias binding.

5) Linings and interfacings, for garment support or insulation — pockets, waistbands, Vilene & wadding.

## Make sure the Components are Safe

Although your product won't actually go on sale in the shops, you still need to show an understanding of certain safety factors. Bear in mind the following questions when you choose your components:

1) Could the component come loose and cause a choking hazard for a child?

2) Are there any sharp edges?

3) Is the fastening secure, yet comfortable to undo?

4) Have I selected components suitable for the intended user?

5) Are any dyes, paints or sparkly bits safe?

*Basically all components you can buy should be safe, but just show that you've thought about the issue.*

## I bet Superman uses Velcro fastenings...

Aren't components fun and exciting? If it all gets too much, run a warm bath, add a few drops of lavender oil, grab a big thick fashion magazine, lie back and relax. You're looking at the components (aren't you), so it's all in the name of research. Who says you can't mix beading with pleasure...

# CAD/CAM

Computers are great for helping you design and manufacture products with speed and accuracy.

## CAD — Computer-Aided Design

1) Computer-Aided Design (CAD) involves _designing products_ on a _computer_, rather than using the traditional methods on paper.

2) CAD software includes _2D painting software_ (e.g. Adobe Photoshop and Corel PHOTO-PAINT), _2D drawing software_ (e.g. Adobe Illustrator and CorelDRAW) and _3D modelling software_ (e.g. ProDESKTOP)

3) You can use CAD to:
- _draw your initial design._
- _draw the pattern pieces for your design._
- _work out how best to lay out your pattern pieces on the material to minimise waste._
- _model your design in 3D — a 'virtual prototype' which will let you see if the design is working._
- _design logos, stencils, fabric patterns and transfers._

_EXAMPLE:_
_Using CAD to design a logo._

## CAM — Computer-Aided Manufacture

1) Computer-Aided Manufacture (CAM) means just what it says — _using computers_ to help with the _manufacture_ of products or components.  _Data_ is _downloaded_ from a _computer_ to a _manufacturing machine_ — and this data _controls_ the way the machine _processes the material_.

2) CAM is usually _linked with CAD_ (this is known as _CAD/CAM_). Products are designed using CAD and then information from the CAD software is used to manufacture the product using CAM.

3) The manufacturing machines used in CAM are _Computer-Numerically Controlled_ (_CNC_).  This means they are sent data in the form of _numbers_ and have an _on-board processor_ which interprets the data.

4) There are _CNC_ versions of _knitting machines_, _embroidery machines_ and _weaving looms_.

_EXAMPLE:  A CNC embroidery machine embroiders the logo._

## CAD/CAM is Quick, Accurate and Efficient

CAD/CAM has many _advantages_:

1) It cuts down on _time_ and _labour_, reducing _costs_.

2) _Different designs_ can be cheaply modelled and _compared_ on-screen.

3) _Changes_ can be made quickly and easily to a design.

4) Designs can be _sent quickly_ to a client or manufacturer via _e-mail_.

5) It is _very accurate_ — which helps ensure a _high-quality_ end product.  Large numbers of _identical products_ can be manufactured quickly and accurately.

But there are some _disadvantages_:

1) The _initial cost_ of software and hardware is high.

2) Workers need _training_ in how to use CAD/CAM and this can be expensive.

3) As with all computer work, _viruses_, _corrupt files_ and _power cuts_ can destroy work.

## There's no escaping computers, not even in a textiles book

CAD and CAM technology is vital to the textiles industry today, and is also due to make another appearance in this book in about 12 pages time.  If you learn this page properly, you'll make your life that little bit easier later on.

# Revision Summary

*Another section over, another Revision Summary to tackle.  Have a go at all the questions below, and if you get any of them wrong, go back through the section and learn those bits again.  It's no use thinking that it'll all come flooding back in the exam, 'cos it won't, not if you don't learn it properly now.  Once you can breeze through all these questions with your eyes closed, your hands tied, and at the same time as you're calculating the exact number of minutes until the exam, you can move on to the next section... Well, OK if you got most of them right...*

1) What are regenerated fibres?

2) Explain how regenerated and synthetic fibres are produced through wet spinning.

3) What is satin weave, and how does it affect the appearance of the fabric?

4) What is linen made from?

5) Name two commonly used regenerated fibres.

6) Name two things that acrylic fabric is used for.

7) Describe the properties of aramid (Kevlar).

8) What is the difference between a mixed fabric and a blended fabric?

9) List three advantages and one disadvantage of using mixtures and blends.

10) Name a fabric which is:
   a) Rainproof, but breathable
   b) Extremely stretchy

11) What can be sewn into other fabrics to make them stronger and stiffer?

12) Describe how fabrics are combined by lamination.

13) List four advantages of chemical dyes over natural dyes.

14) Which type of fabric absorbs dyes better; natural fabrics or synthetic fabrics?

15) Describe how batik dying is carried out.

16) List three disadvantages of roller printing.

17) Name the fastest and most commonly used method of printing on fabrics.

18) What is appliqué?

19) Name three embroidery stitches.

20) List four reasons why a fabric may be given a finish.

21) What kind of finish could be applied to a fabric to make it crease resistant?

22) What does ITCLC stand for?

23) What does this symbol mean when it appears on a clothes label?

24) Name five different types of component.

25) List five things you should consider when choosing your components.

26) Describe the main advantages of using CAD (without peaking at the opposite page).

27) List three things that can be controlled by CAM.

# Product Analysis

Manufacturers spend time and effort researching their goods before production.
If you take a close look at what they've done, it can give you useful information that will help with your own design.

## Product Analysis — Looking at Products in Detail

1) As a consumer you analyse products all the time. You might choose T-shirt A instead of T-shirt B because it has a <u>better logo</u>, or the fabric <u>feels nicer</u>, or it <u>fits more comfortably</u>.

2) Proper product analysis is a similar process, but in rather more <u>depth</u>.
   These are the major points you need to look at:

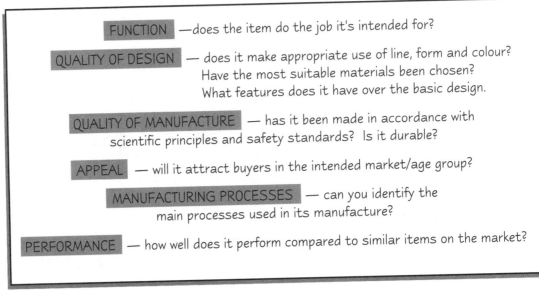

FUNCTION —does the item do the job it's intended for?

QUALITY OF DESIGN — does it make appropriate use of line, form and colour?
Have the most suitable materials been chosen?
What features does it have over the basic design.

QUALITY OF MANUFACTURE — has it been made in accordance with
scientific principles and safety standards? Is it durable?

APPEAL — will it attract buyers in the intended market/age group?

MANUFACTURING PROCESSES — can you identify the
main processes used in its manufacture?

PERFORMANCE — how well does it perform compared to similar items on the market?

3) The trick to doing product analysis is to <u>pick through</u> the bulk of information for just those bits which are relevant to you.

## Analyse Other People's Products to Get Good Ideas for Your Own

1) Analysing products means you can take advantage of all the research <u>already done</u> by manufacturers.

2) It can save you <u>time</u>, <u>effort</u> and <u>money</u> by avoiding costly mistakes.

3) You can analyse how a product has <u>developed over time</u> and look at the <u>current trends</u>.

4) It can guide your decision making and help you to select the <u>best materials</u> and <u>method for making</u> your product.

5) You can get information from <u>various sources</u>:

Books   Magazines   Trade journals
Leaflets   Internet   Questionnaires and Surveys

## Present Your Findings Using Charts, Diagrams, Photos...

Vary the way you present your findings — a <u>chart</u> or <u>diagram</u> is often better than a paragraph of writing.
Use various <u>colouring methods</u> to enhance your work.
Include <u>graphs</u> and <u>questionnaires</u> as well as <u>photographs</u>, <u>scanned images</u>, and <u>drawings</u>.

## Analyse, don't plagiarise

Going through other people's designs can be really, really useful — you can see where they went wrong, and how they solved the same problems you're facing with your product. However, you need to avoid coming out with the same tired old ideas that everyone else has already used. Originality will get you better marks.

# Ambience and Harmony

Ambience and harmony — nothing to do with music (at least not in this case).
It's about the total effect created by your design in terms of colour, texture, line and so on.

## Ambience is the Overall Effect of a Design

Ambience (sometimes called "aesthetics") is the overall effect achieved by all the elements of a design.
The design might be a clothing item, an interior design for a room, or a complete make-over for a company.
Many factors come together to create the right feeling for a project.

Colour
schemes

Texture
and
pattern

Variation
in
surfaces

To achieve a good ambience you need to pay attention to:

1) *PATTERN*   Lines on a product can change how it appears — e.g. vertical lines on a shirt
make you look taller and slimmer, while horizontal lines make you look shorter and fatter.
Lines also alter the impression of space within a room, visually adding height or width.

2) *CUT/FIT*   Create different moods by adjusting the cut of garments. For example, a sharply cut, closely
fitting garment creates a disciplined ambience, suitable for uniforms and clothes for office
workers. A floaty or baggy cut is more suited to leisure clothing.

3) *COLOUR*   Colours play a big part in creating the overall mood.
Different uses of colours can make a products look heavy, light or stand out.

## Harmony — Everything Working Together

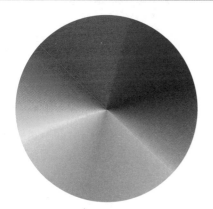

Harmony is when all the parts of a design adapt well and work together,
creating a relaxed and comfortable ambience.

An essential ingredient is getting the colour harmony right.
Too many colours can be confusing — too few can be too dull.

1) *MONOCHROME HARMONY*
Using tints and shades of the same colour.

2) *RELATED HARMONY*
Using small bands of colours next to each other on the colour wheel.

3) *CONTRAST HARMONY*
Using colours which are opposite to each other on the colour wheel.

## Ambience and Harmony is Important for Corporate Identity

Corporate identity plays a major role in influencing consumer choice — it's important to get it right.
The identity is created by uniforms, logos, packaging and interiors — textiles products are vital.
The designer can intentionally alter the way you see a company.

1) *DARKER COLOURS* are used to suggest authority.
2) *LIGHTER SHADES* are less threatening and encourage more interaction with clients.
3) *BRIGHT COLOURS* are likely to denote fun, leisure and a younger image.

## We're a young, fun, groovy towel manufacturer

Apart from being really interesting places full of slug pellets and grouting, DIY super stores can be a great source
of inspiration when it comes to designing interiors. If you've got some free time, pop in and look at all the cool stuff
they sell. Or, watch one of the thousands of DIY programmes on telly everyday — you can't miss them (I've tried).

# Development and Evaluation

Before you start designing your product, make sure you've sorted out these things:

1) the <u>design brief</u>　　　3) <u>who</u> you are designing for (your <u>target market</u>)

2) the <u>specification</u>　　　4) <u>what</u> you are designing (your <u>product</u>)

## Develop your Rough Ideas into Detailed Designs

**INITIAL DESIGNS**

Initial designs (thumbnail sketches) are done <u>quickly</u>.
Experiment with <u>styles</u>, <u>shapes</u> and <u>patterns</u> taken from your research.
Try "<u>think doodling</u>" — it's like brainstorming all your ideas on a page.

In industry, designers will start with a <u>mood board</u> — a collection of photographs, magazine pictures, fabric samples or anything to inspire the theme.

**DEVELOPING IDEAS**

Focus on a few specific ideas that you want to <u>develop</u>. Do fairly detailed sketches for these. Take more <u>time and care</u>, add <u>colour</u> and <u>shading</u> (don't use felt tips — they don't look very good).

You may decide you need a <u>working drawing</u> (see page 7).
This is a detailed, annotated (labelled) drawing of a product.
Label <u>fabrics</u>, <u>components</u> and <u>sizes</u>. Produce a <u>3D</u> sketch if possible (this is where you could use CAD, see p.22, 40-41).

## Make Samples to Test and Evaluate the Design

Get the sewing machine out and produce <u>samples</u> of <u>decorative techniques</u>, <u>seams</u>, etc for your design.
<u>Check</u> to make sure the samples match the original <u>design criteria</u> (design brief and specification).

## A Prototype is a Full-Scale Model of the Product

Once you're clear about what you're making it's a good idea to make a <u>model</u> of your product.
This is called a "<u>prototype</u>" (in fashion called a "<u>toile</u>").
In industry, a prototype clothing item would be made from <u>cheap calico</u> (plain white cotton fabric) and modifications would be made following <u>surveys</u> and <u>questionnaires</u> to check whether or not the target market like it.

## <u>Follow these handy design tips...</u>

1) <u>Brainstorm</u> and draw <u>simple designs</u> (doodles) at first. Don't worry about being neat at this stage.

2) Take your <u>best bits</u> and <u>add detail</u>.

3) <u>Trace body outlines</u> if you need to for fashion sketches.

4) Use a fineliner to <u>highlight detail</u>.

5) Use "<u>exploded diagrams</u>" to show extra details of the <u>construction</u> and <u>decoration</u>.

6) Keep checking back and asking yourself "<u>Does my product meet my design criteria</u>?"

7) Review your work <u>often</u> and don't be afraid to <u>modify</u> if you feel that something isn't working.

# Quality Assurance and Control

Quality Assurance (QA) is all about <u>standards</u> — <u>setting standards</u> and meeting them.
Quality Control (QC) is how you <u>check</u> that you're meeting those standards.

## Quality Assurance (QA) — Setting and Meeting Standards

Quality Assurance is a system that is set up to <u>make sure</u> a product meets all the points on the <u>specification</u>.
An important part of QA is Quality Control...

## Quality Control (QC) — Checking the Product

1) Quality Control is the process of <u>checking</u> and <u>inspecting</u> the product and making sure it meets all the points on the <u>specification</u>.

2) Checks may be carried out at <u>any point</u> in manufacture. A <u>sample product</u> will be checked when it is being made. The checks can be made <u>visually</u> or using a <u>computer</u>.

3) If any faults are found, <u>changes</u> will be made to improve the manufacturing process.

4) A factory usually has a <u>Quality Control Department</u> which oversees all the inspections and testing. It will make sure that the right controls are in place to ensure a quality product.

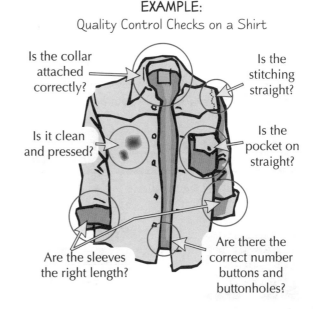

EXAMPLE:
Quality Control Checks on a Shirt

Is the collar attached correctly?

Is the stitching straight?

Is it clean and pressed?

Is the pocket on straight?

Are the sleeves the right length?

Are there the correct number buttons and buttonholes?

## Tolerances are the Margin of Error

The manufacturer will allow certain <u>tolerances</u> within the manufacture.
These are <u>maximum</u> or <u>minimum</u> limits allowed, usually for the size of a part of the product.

e.g. the length of the hem on a shirt could be between 1.5 cm and 1.8 cm.

## Quality Control is Worth the Effort

Good Quality Control takes time and effort, but it's <u>well worth it</u>. These are the benefits:

1) Less <u>wastage</u> of materials and worker have to <u>repeat less</u> work.
2) These both result in <u>lower costs</u> for the company.
3) Good products give the company a <u>good reputation</u>, which means more <u>customers</u>.

## Kwolity contröll — essenshul...

Don't get QA and QC mixed up — Quality Assurance is the big picture about the standards that have been set for a product, and Quality Control is the nuts and bolts of actually checking the products.

# Target Market

Your target market is about who, exactly, you're going to design for. This may be an individual, a small group, or a very wide band of people. There's no point guessing, or thinking that people will like something just because you do.

## Research — Find Out About Your Target Market

1) By <u>asking questions</u> about your target users, you can get a <u>clearer idea</u> of how your product needs to perform.

2) First, you need to decide exactly <u>who</u> your product is aimed at. What age range is it aimed at... is it going to be gender-specific... etc.

3) Some products will have a very <u>specific</u> target user, e.g. a bag designed for teenagers who use wheelchairs.

4) Once you know who your target users are, think about what <u>they'll need</u> from the product. E.g. does it need to be lightweight... should it be waterproof... should it use bright or dull colours... does the user need a clasp that's easily undone?

*(These are limited examples — do a brainstorm to come up with lots more of your own.)*

*HINT #47: People who live in the Arctic may not have a pressing need for skimpy swimwear.*

## Use a Variety of Sources for Your Research

Get information on <u>consumer choice</u> (i.e. what's already out there) from as many of these sources as you can:

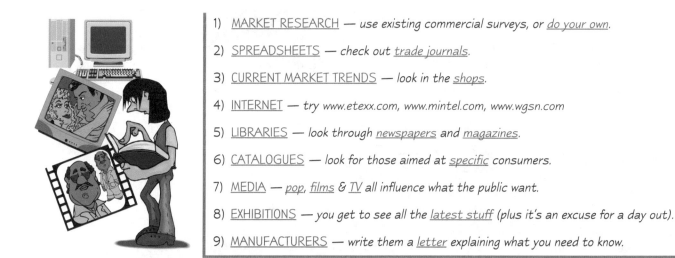

1) <u>MARKET RESEARCH</u> — *use existing commercial surveys, or <u>do your own</u>.*

2) <u>SPREADSHEETS</u> — *check out <u>trade journals</u>.*

3) <u>CURRENT MARKET TRENDS</u> — *look in the <u>shops</u>.*

4) <u>INTERNET</u> — *try www.etexx.com, www.mintel.com, www.wgsn.com*

5) <u>LIBRARIES</u> — *look through <u>newspapers</u> and <u>magazines</u>.*

6) <u>CATALOGUES</u> — *look for those aimed at <u>specific</u> consumers.*

7) <u>MEDIA</u> — *<u>pop</u>, <u>films</u> & <u>TV</u> all influence what the public want.*

8) <u>EXHIBITIONS</u> — *you get to see all the <u>latest stuff</u> (plus it's an excuse for a day out).*

9) <u>MANUFACTURERS</u> — *write them a <u>letter</u> explaining what you need to know.*

## Presenting Your Findings — Be Creative

Even if your project is really dull, it doesn't mean you have to bore everyone else too — <u>be creative</u> when you <u>present</u> your information. Try any of these:

1) Use a combination of <u>sketches</u> and <u>notes</u>.
2) Use <u>text</u> along with <u>photos</u>, <u>clippings</u> and <u>graphs</u>.
3) Combine <u>spreadsheets</u>, <u>graphs</u> and <u>charts</u> to show off your <u>IT skills</u>.

## *I only bought these £70 jeans so that I could research the stitching...*(honest)

Keep your research relevant — it doesn't matter how fond you are of lycra, it's no use researching beach wear when you're designing for Eskimos. They don't like swimming anyway. The internet is a great place to find stuff out, especially if you're making something obscure that isn't in many shops or text books (fur bikinis perhaps).

# People's Choices

It's easy to think you make your own choices. In fact there are many things that influence the decisions you make.

## Social Trends — People are Affected by What They See Around Them

*An extreme example — dressing like Elvis Presley.*

*This man seems to be dressed like Bill Clinton.*

*The sad result of social trends — dressing like a ninny.*

All kinds of factors can influence what you wear:

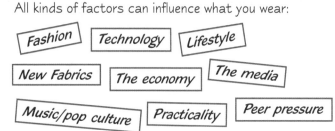

Fashion · Technology · Lifestyle · New Fabrics · The economy · The media · Music/pop culture · Practicality · Peer pressure

Some fashion trends are very <u>short-lived</u>, perhaps only lasting a <u>few months</u>. Others <u>catch on</u> and remain in use for a <u>long time</u>. Designers and manufacturers are <u>well aware</u> of this and adjust their <u>marketing</u> to take advantage of it.

## Cultural Influences Affect Your Choices

<u>Cultural differences</u> play a crucial role in people's choices. What might be acceptable in <u>one culture</u> would be frowned on in <u>another</u>. <u>Religious beliefs</u> can influence people's ideas about what's acceptable. <u>Style</u>, <u>colours</u> and <u>patterns</u> can all have cultural significance.

*A Buddhist monk.*

## Moral Issues — I Don't Wear Kitten Fur

Many people will choose not to use or wear certain products for moral reasons. Examples include:

Products tested on <u>animals</u>;
Wearing animal <u>fur</u>;
Companies that use <u>child labour</u> to produce products cheaply.

## Many People Care About Environmental Issues

<u>Environmental issues</u> in textiles production include:

1) Use of <u>pesticides</u> to increase cotton crop yields.
2) Development of <u>GM crops</u>.
3) Environmental impact of industrial <u>pollution</u> and <u>waste disposal</u>.
4) Preservation of <u>natural resources</u>.
5) <u>Recycling</u> of materials.
6) Excessive <u>packaging</u> being used on products.

It's often difficult for a <u>consumer</u> to know if a <u>manufacturer</u> has acted in the best interests of the environment. In many cases it's down to <u>pressure groups</u> and <u>governments</u> to ensure that the <u>correct procedures</u> are followed. However, <u>consumers</u> can have an effect by <u>boycotting</u> products or companies that don't play by the rules.

## <u>Look, I wear this long brown robe and laser-sword for religious reasons...</u>

Fashion is a crazy thing that makes you buy stuff you don't need, and in six months, won't want. Remember, contentment is not about having what you want; it's about wanting what you have. Wise words (though I think "Excitement?... Adventure?... A Jedi craves not these things" is more useful as a life statement).

# Consumer Rights

By law, a consumer has the right to be sold quality goods, and to return goods and get a refund if they don't meet quality standards. You need to think about these rights when you design and make any textiles product.

## The Trades Description Act Means You Can't Lie About Products

The <u>Trades Description Act</u> means that any claim a manufacturer makes about their product must be <u>true</u>.

It applies to what they say about:

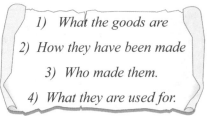

*1) What the goods are*

*2) How they have been made*

*3) Who made them.*

*4) What they are used for.*

It also bans <u>false price reductions</u>, and means that a trader can't give <u>false information</u> about what they sell in <u>writing</u>, <u>verbally</u> or in an <u>advertisement</u>.

## The Consumer Safety Act Means Things Have to Be Safe

1) This law gives the government the power to <u>ban</u> or <u>control</u> the sale of <u>dangerous</u> or <u>potentially dangerous</u> goods.

2) It also covers regulation of <u>fire</u> and <u>safety hazards</u> for <u>children's nightwear</u>, <u>anoraks</u> and <u>fabric toys</u>.

3) Children's nightwear must be <u>treated</u> to make the fabric less flammable. <u>All nightwear</u> must display the warning "<u>Keep away from fire</u>".

## Furniture and Furnishings Must Meet Fire Safety Regulations

1) The <u>Fire Safety Regulations</u> apply to both <u>new</u> and <u>second-hand</u> goods.

2) They say that all <u>fabrics/padding</u> used to cover or make <u>furniture</u> must be <u>resistant</u> to "<u>smouldering from cigarette ignition</u>" (won't catch fire from burning fags). It applies to <u>sofas</u> and <u>soft furnishings</u> such as cushions, pillows and loose furnishings.

3) Furniture should contain <u>warnings</u> about potential fire risks or labels to show they have passed <u>safety tests</u>.

## Sale and Supply of Goods Act 1979 Applies to Mail Order Goods

The <u>Sale and Supply of Goods Act 1979</u> protects consumers when they buy goods. The goods must <u>fit the description</u>, be of <u>satisfactory quality</u> and be <u>fit for purpose</u>. This protects you when you buy a product from a <u>mail order catalogue</u> — the product they send <u>must</u> fit the description in the catalogue.

## <u>Excuse me... is this toy lion meant to have 6 inch, razor-sharp, metal teeth?</u>

Consumer regulations are there to protect you from evil retailers trying to rip you off. It's really handy to know all the stuff on this page, so that you know when you're entitled to a refund — plus you've got the small matter of an exam to take, remember? You better read it over again then, hadn't you?

# Health and Safety Issues

Health and Safety must be considered at all points during the designing and making of your textile product. You must ensure your product will be <u>safe to use</u> and <u>safe to make</u>.

## The Product must be Safe to Use

<u>Every</u> textile product must be <u>safe to use</u> — it's the designer's job to <u>make sure</u> it is. Some products carry <u>symbols</u> to show that the product has passed certain <u>quality/safety checks</u>.

The <u>British Standards Institution</u> (BSI) sets <u>safety standards</u> for a range of products — things like <u>crash helmets</u>, <u>prams</u> and <u>toys</u> for small children and products made from <u>flame-resistant materials</u>. If a product meets its standards then it'll carry the <u>Kitemark</u>.

## The Product must be Safe to Make

The <u>Health and Safety at Work Act</u> means employers are <u>legally responsible</u> for the Health and Safety of their <u>employees</u>. It also makes <u>employees</u> responsible for <u>using</u> the <u>safety equipment</u> provided for them *(see page 34)*.

The four main areas to look at are:
1) The design of the machines and tools being used.
2) The layout of the work area.
3) The training of the workforce.
4) The safety devices and procedures.

There are a number of <u>regulations</u> and <u>codes of practice</u> which must be considered when setting up a manufacturing system. They cover things like:
1) The safe use of machinery.
2) The use of protective clothing and equipment.
3) The use of computer screens.
4) The carrying of goods by hand.

## Make Sure You Keep Yourself Safe

When working in a textiles workshop <u>you</u> need to <u>look after yourself</u>.
1) Wear <u>protective clothing</u>, such as aprons, gloves and goggles, when necessary.
2) Tie back <u>long hair</u>.
3) Make sure you are not wearing any <u>loose clothing</u> or <u>jewellery</u>.
4) Make sure there is <u>good ventilation</u> when using <u>chemicals</u>, <u>paints</u> or <u>glues</u>.
5) Use <u>machine guards</u> on dangerous machines.
6) <u>Take care</u> when using <u>hot water</u> or <u>irons</u>.
7) Keep work areas <u>tidy</u>.
8) Use and carry <u>sharp tools</u> carefully.

## SAFETY WARNING: *Some needles 5and scissors may be sharp...*

Back in my day, we played catch with hot irons, and shook our long flowing locks in the face of sewing machines. Then again, most of us now have missing fingers and hideous scars. Best stick to the safety regulations, eh... And it's not just flesh-ripping, blood-spurting injuries you've got to worry about — don't forget the dangers of RSI and eye strain.

# Risk Assessment

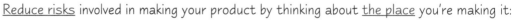

When you design and make a textiles product you have to look at what might harm people in these areas:
a) raw materials   b) manufacturing processes   c) working practices.
If there are any problems, you have to work out how to reduce or eliminate the risk.

## You Have to Reduce and Minimise Risks

Reduce risks involved in making your product by thinking about the place you're making it:

1) Think about the layout of the room.
   There must be enough space around each machine.
   Walkways and exits must always be kept clear.

2) There must be enough light — if possible it should be natural light.

3) The temperature should be comfortable.

4) There must be ventilation — especially if you are using chemicals.

5) Workers using noisy machinery for a long time must wear ear protection.

## You Have to Complete a "Risk Assessment"

The Health and Safety at Work Act says that businesses must complete a risk assessment for each stage of production.

The risk assessment will point out what must be done for the work area to meet the Health and Safety standards.

The results of the assessment have to be checked by a Health and Safety Inspector.

> The risk assessment looks at:
> 1) The layout of the work area.
> 2) Dust and fume extraction.
> 3) The use and storage of chemicals.
> 4) Safety procedures for using machinery.

## The Textiles Industry Can Harm the Environment

These are some of the environmental problems which can be caused by the textiles industry:

1) Using a lot of energy.

2) Pollution of air (contributing to global warming).

3) Pollution of water.

4) Problems with the disposal of waste and used products.

The harmful effects of making textiles products can be reduced if you:

1) Use unbleached, organic, natural materials.

2) Using modern, less toxic dyes.

3) Re-use waste water to make dyes.

4) Use recycled products — e.g. recycled plastic bottles used to make fleece fabrics.

---

**SAFETY WARNING:** *If your ears are bleeding, the machinery may be too loud...*

Read and enjoy... You'll need to know all this stuff when you've built your massive textiles empire, and you're employing thousands of people worldwide. Remember, fighting those lawsuits and handing out compensation to injured workers can be expensive. Not to mention the fines for killing all those fish...

# Domestic Equipment

When you make your product it's important to use the <u>right equipment</u> for each job.

## *Always use the Right Scissors for the Job*

1) Use <u>dressmaking scissors</u> to cut <u>fabric</u>. These have long, very sharp blades.
2) Use <u>embroidery scissors</u> for <u>small</u> work with stitches.
3) Use <u>pinking shears</u> to cut fabric with a <u>zigzag edge</u> — this helps prevent fabric from fraying.
4) Use <u>paper scissors</u> to cut <u>patterns</u>. <u>Craft knives</u> can be used to cut stencils.

## *Join Fabric using Pins, Sewing Machines, Overlockers...*

You can <u>join</u> fabric with <u>temporary</u> or <u>permanent</u> joins.

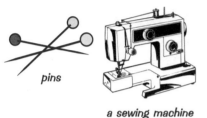

*pins*

*a sewing machine*

1) <u>Pins</u> — temporary, hold pieces of fabric together before stitching.
2) <u>Tacking stitch</u> — a temporary join usually done with cheap thread. Stitches are about 1 cm long.
3) <u>Machine lockstitch</u> — a permanent join. A basic sewing machine can produce a range of stitches. A computerised sewing machine can produce more stitches at the touch of a button.

After joining your fabric you'll have to <u>finish the edges</u> to make it look neat and to prevent fraying. You can do this in a number of ways.

1) Use a <u>special seam</u> (e.g. French seam).
2) Cut the fabric with <u>pinking shears</u>.
3) Use an <u>overlocker</u> to give a professional finish. This machine joins, trims and neatens the edge of the fabric to prevent it from fraying.

French seam

Overlocked seam

## *Use Computerised Equipment to add Embroidery*

1) You can add decorative stitching (<u>embroidery</u>) using <u>CAD</u> (Computer Aided Design) and <u>CAM</u> (Computer Aided Manufacture).
   *A number of machines can do this — e.g. the Janome Memory Craft, POEM and Pfaff Creative.*

2) CAM machines can <u>stitch designs</u> already programmed in the machine or you can use <u>special software</u> to produce your own designs (CAD).
   *CAD designs are usually saved to a disk/memory card so they can be transferred to the CAM machine.*

3) The <u>needle</u> stays in the <u>same place</u> and the machine moves the fabric around in an <u>embroidery hoop</u>.
   *When you've finished your product you may want to make a label using a CAD package.*

## *Iron your Product to Improve its Shape and Appearance*

1) <u>Dry irons</u> use a combination of <u>heat and pressure</u> to press creases out of the fabric.
2) <u>Steam irons</u> also use <u>water/steam</u> to make it easier to remove creases.

## Q: What's harder than trying to find a needle in a haystack?

This is all really useful practical stuff that you'll need to know when you actually come to make things.
Make sure you learn all the ways to join material together, and why different methods are better for different jobs.
And remember, take ALL the pins out of your garment BEFORE you get your friend try it for size...

# Industrial Equipment

In a <u>factory</u>, processes are completed on a <u>massive scale</u>. They use special equipment to work at <u>high speed</u>.

## They Cut Fabric with Water and Sew Without People

1) Factories use computer-controlled machines to cut through <u>many layers</u> of fabric at once.

2) They cut fabric at high speed using <u>vertical knives</u>, <u>high-pressure water jets</u> or <u>laser beams</u>.

3) Industrial sewing machines are very strong as they need to work at <u>high speeds</u>.
There are different machines specially designed for each process in making the product.
Automatic machines are used for specialist functions like buttonholes and sewing on buttons.
Fully-automated machines are used for repeated processes and provide <u>consistent quality</u>.

4) These machines <u>don't need people to work them</u> — just a few staff to monitor the work.

## CAD/CAM Embroidery Machines come in Different Flavours

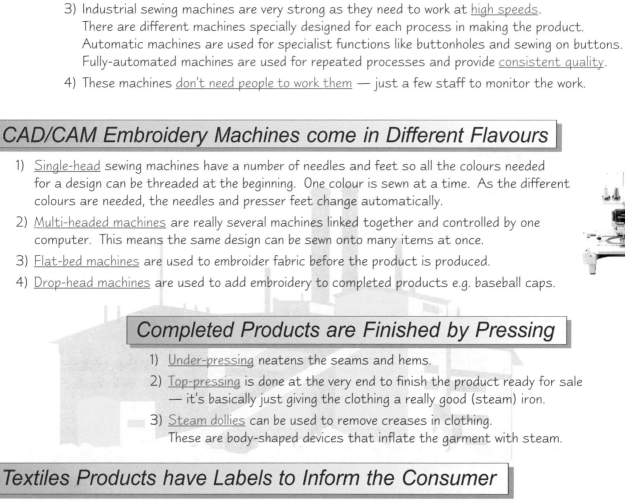

1) <u>Single-head</u> sewing machines have a number of needles and feet so all the colours needed for a design can be threaded at the beginning. One colour is sewn at a time. As the different colours are needed, the needles and presser feet change automatically.

2) <u>Multi-headed machines</u> are really several machines linked together and controlled by one computer. This means the same design can be sewn onto many items at once.

3) <u>Flat-bed machines</u> are used to embroider fabric before the product is produced.

4) <u>Drop-head machines</u> are used to add embroidery to completed products e.g. baseball caps.

## Completed Products are Finished by Pressing

1) <u>Under-pressing</u> neatens the seams and hems.

2) <u>Top-pressing</u> is done at the very end to finish the product ready for sale
— it's basically just giving the clothing a really good (steam) iron.

3) <u>Steam dollies</u> can be used to remove creases in clothing.
These are body-shaped devices that inflate the garment with steam.

## Textiles Products have Labels to Inform the Consumer

Some information has to be there <u>by law</u> (e.g. the fibre content and any safety warnings).
Other information is <u>voluntary</u> (e.g. size and care instructions — see pg 20).
<u>Packaging</u> is often used to help retailers display textile products and to promote the brand name.

## The Health and Safety at Work Act 1974 means that...

EMPLOYERS MUST:
1) provide safety training
2) maintain machines
3) provide a safety policy
4) provide first aid facilities

EMPLOYEES:
Employees are responsible for using the safety equipment provided.
They must make sure they use the safety guards on machines and that protective clothing is worn e.g. chain mail gloves for cutting machines.

## *Revenge of the Multi-Headed Machines — one to miss at the Multiplex...*

This stuff is all about making products in lightning-quick time so that the fat cats who own the businesses get much more money quicker. Still, even they've got to make sure that everything's completely safe for the workers.

# Different Types of Production

There are different ways of making things, depending on how many products you're going to make.

## One-off Production is When You Make a Single Unique Product

One-off production (or "job production") is where one item is made.
It's made by one person, or by a small team all working on parts of the same item.
The finished product is unique — e.g. a wedding dress for a particular woman.
The main features of one-off production are:

1) Usually it's for high quality products.
2) Each item takes a lot of time to make.
3) It needs skilled workers.
4) The machinery used should be able to be adapted to a number of processes.
5) It's more expensive than batch or mass produced items (see below).

## Batch Production is Making a Small Number of Identical Products

1) Batch production is used to make a relatively small number of identical products, e.g. 100 Santa hats.
2) Machines can be altered after each batch.
   This means that the manufacturer can react to specific orders and a variety of styles can be made.
3) Production costs are less than in one-off production because more than one product is made.
   Also, a batch could be repeated in future.
4) Staff have flexible working conditions and are trained to deal with different batches.

## Mass Production is for Large Numbers of Products

Mass production (or "volume production") is used when large quantities
of an identical product are to be made. There are three types:

### In-Line Production

1) *Work passes through a series of stations.*
   *At each station a worker performs a particular job on identical pieces, over and over again.*
2) *Suitable for making large numbers of products for large retailers.*

### Repetitive Flow

*This produces large numbers of identical products for a relatively low cost.*
*The production is broken down into sub assembly lines making smaller parts of the product, e.g. a sleeve.*
*This process is expensive to set up initially but mass production leads to lower costs because:*

1) *Materials can be bought in bulk.*
2) *Semi-skilled or unskilled labour can be used.*
3) *The high cost of machines is spread out over a large number of products.*
4) *The process can be fully automated.*

### Continual Flow

*This is the same as repetitive flow, but assembly lines run 24 hours a day, 7 days a week — it's expensive to shut down and start up. Continual flow can be used to make things like dish cloths or tights.*

## Now I know all about repetitive flow...

...but continual flow is where it's at. The author Jack Kerouac had a good technique — he'd feed a stupidly long roll of paper into his typewriter and just type continuously for days — bet most of it was pants, though.

*SECTION THREE — DESIGN AND MARKET INFLUENCES*

# More Production Processes

When choosing a production method for your textiles product, you have to think about these things:

1) Will all the <u>materials</u> and <u>components</u> be available for you to use when you need to use them?
2) Who is your <u>target market</u>?
3) Will they pay a lot of money for a <u>one-off</u> item? Will they be looking for a <u>low-cost</u>, <u>mass-produced</u> item?

## The Just-in-Time System — Regular Small Deliveries

In a <u>Just-in-time</u> (JIT) system a manufacturer gets the <u>materials</u> and <u>components</u> delivered <u>regularly</u> in <u>small amounts</u> and uses them as soon as they're delivered. These are the <u>advantages</u>:

1) Saves on the <u>cost</u> of <u>storing</u> materials and less money <u>tied-up</u> in stock.
2) Production <u>speeds up</u>.

BUT, <u>Materials</u> and <u>components</u> have to be delivered <u>fault free</u> (there's no time to return goods).

## Off-the-Peg Clothes are Cheaper

"<u>Off-the-peg</u>" clothes are bought <u>ready-to-wear</u> from a shop.
These items are <u>cheaper</u> because they're made to <u>standard sizes</u>.
<u>Templates</u> are made for different sizes, and a <u>batch</u> of products is made in each size — this <u>reduces costs</u>.

## Fancy, Expensive — That's Haute Couture

<u>Haute Couture</u> is a French term relating to <u>one-off</u> fashion design, usually by a <u>designer fashion house</u> (e.g. Alexander McQueen or Vivienne Westwood).
These clothes are made from the <u>highest quality fabrics</u> which can cost thousands of pounds.
They usually make clothes for a <u>small number</u> of <u>very wealthy</u> people.

## Computer-Aided Manufacture Can Speed Things Up

<u>Computer-Aided Manufacture</u> (or CAM) means using computers to help with the making of a product.
*For example, a <u>computer</u> could work out the <u>most economical layplan</u> for
bulk cutting fabric and then <u>download</u> this information to an automated fabric cutter.*

CIM is <u>Computer Integrated Manufacture</u>. It means the production system is <u>fully automated</u> (i.e. CAD and CAM are used). This helps the designers and office staff keep track of the manufacturing process.

These are the good things about using <u>computers</u>:

1) Computers help <u>speed up</u> production.
2) Fewer workers are needed, so they <u>lower the cost</u> over a period of time.
3) They're <u>more accurate</u> than people.
4) The <u>quality</u> of the final product can be <u>higher</u>.

## ..........................................................................Wait!  Just in time for a gag...

As experts at the just-in-time system of production, we at CGP make it a policy to get our books onto the shelves 3 minutes before the customer walks in and buys one. We're working on a Haute Couture range too — fancy your very own one-of-a-kind revision guide on sloth-baiting? It'll cost you an arm and a leg, but we'll write you one...

# Systems and Control

'Systems and Control' is about the ins and outs of getting something produced.
The better the system, the quicker you'll get to the end product.

## A Production System is the Whole System That Makes A Product

A <u>production system</u> is the <u>whole system</u> that goes into <u>making a product</u>.
Think of it as a <u>chain</u> of materials, events and components that <u>link together</u>.

A <u>Production Manager</u>'s job is to make sure the system is <u>working</u>
and find ways to make it <u>even more efficient</u>. Each manager studies
just <u>part</u> of the organisation — this is call a "<u>System Boundary</u>".

## Making a Product Involves Inputs, Transformation and Outputs

<u>INPUTS GO IN</u> — they come from the <u>client</u>, the <u>designer</u>, the <u>materials</u>
  and the <u>employer</u>.

<u>TRANSFORMATION</u> — the inputs are <u>transformed</u>.
  Transformations include:
  <u>pattern layout</u>, <u>cutting</u>, <u>construction</u>, <u>finishing</u> and <u>checking</u>.

<u>OUTPUTS</u> — what you get at the other end (the finished product).
  Outputs include:
  the <u>finished item</u>, <u>waste materials</u>, <u>paid employees</u>, <u>satisfied customers</u>, etc.

> <u>EXAMPLE: A FURRY WINTER BIKINI</u>
>
> <u>INPUTS =</u>
> research and materials such as the fur
>
> <u>TRANSFORMATIONS =</u>
> creating the product in the factory
>
> <u>OUTPUTS =</u>
> "furkini" sold in shops, employees paid,
> Brighton much busier this January.

## Feedback and Control — Checking Things are Working

<u>Systems analysis</u> is checking a particular part of the process to see
whether or not it's working efficiently and whether it could be improved.

<u>Feedback</u> is information that is passed back from a later stage in a system to an earlier stage.
It's important for making improvements by changing the input, or by altering the process.

> *<u>The Important Parts of Feedback and Control</u>:*
>
> 1) <u>Time</u>, <u>energy</u>, <u>cost</u> and <u>efficiency</u> all have to be carefully considered.
>
> 2) <u>Flow charts</u> are used to demonstrate best sequences of work.
>
> 3) <u>Time plans</u> are important — remember time is money.
>
> 4) <u>Process diagrams</u> and <u>block diagrams</u> show availability of materials, order of work etc.
>
> 5) Suitable <u>software</u> should be used if it saves time.
>
> 6) <u>Feedback loops</u> and <u>critical checks</u> should be included to ensure consistent quality.
>
> 7) <u>Quantity</u> has to be <u>balanced</u> against <u>quality</u>.

## *I felt really ill yesterday — then I got my foodback...*

Feedback lets you know you're doing a good job. Imagine if you handed in your project and never heard anything more
about it ever... actually, that sounds perfect... You've got to learn from feedback and change it for next time.

# Setting Up Your Own System

Few plans are foolproof — but the better your production plan, the better your end product will be.

## Start at the Beginning

Before you start your production plan you need information about:

a) the <u>type</u> and <u>quantity</u> of <u>materials</u> and <u>components</u> you need,

b) the <u>processes</u> involved and the <u>estimated time</u> each stage will take,

c) a list of the <u>equipment</u> you need,

d) <u>possible problems</u> that might occur.

## Plan Out Your Production Processes

1) Draw up your production sequence as a <u>flow chart</u> or <u>block diagram</u>.

2) Include the following details about the <u>manufacturing process</u>:
   storage    operations    inspections    movement

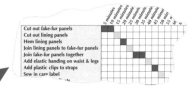

3) Draw up a <u>Gantt chart</u> to make sure each stage runs to the correct <u>time schedule</u> (see page 8).

4) Allow time for <u>checking</u> and <u>re-working</u> if a process fails to come up to standard.

## A Sub Assembly Needs Its Own Production Plan

A sub assembly is a part of your product which is <u>made separately</u> and so needs its <u>own production plan</u>.

For example: <u>dying fabric</u> or <u>creating an embroidered logo</u> would be seen as sub assemblies.

The sub assembly may be made in a different location, such as a manufacturing cell, or be bought pre-made.

## Quality Control Stops You Making Rubbish

Look at <u>samples</u> of items in your production.
<u>Analyse</u> and <u>record</u> any <u>faults</u> you find.
Sort out problems as you go — don't wait until the end.
Don't forget to check the quality of <u>manufactured components</u> before you use them.

Faults may be put into these categories:
1) <u>CRITICAL</u> — failing to meet the <u>specification</u>.  The item may have to be <u>rejected</u>.
2) <u>MAJOR</u> — usually a <u>sewing fault</u>.  The item can be <u>re-worked</u>.
3) <u>MINOR</u> — a <u>trivial flaw</u> that falls within <u>tolerances</u>.
          Tolerances are the <u>acceptable limits</u> within which you must work.

## Barry Norman says he hates Spiderman — now that's a critical fault...

The best thing about quality control is that all the items with minor faults (like a bit of stitching that's wonky) get sold off at bargain-bucket prices.  I haven't got one item of clothing with straight stitching...

# Batch / Mass Production

Most products you make in school will be one-off products, e.g. a single hat or cushion. But sometimes you'll have to design and make a group of identical products (batch production) — and this needs careful planning.

## Design your Product to be Suitable for Batch / Mass Production

When you're <u>designing</u> a product for batch/mass production:

1) Choose materials, components and equipment which are <u>easily available</u> and <u>affordable</u>.
2) <u>Avoid</u> labour-intensive processes, e.g. hand embroidery.
3) <u>Avoid</u> processes which need highly-skilled workers.
4) Design clothes in <u>standard sizes</u> (so they're more marketable).
5) Keep designs unfussy, with <u>no unnecessary parts</u> or features.
6) Think about <u>how your design could be varied</u> in different batches, e.g. different colours and decorations.
7) Think about whether <u>automated machinery</u> could be used to make production quicker.

## Create a Detailed Production Plan for Making Your Product

Your production plan should include:

- the <u>scale/type of production</u> that is going to be used (see page 35)
- the <u>sequence of tasks</u> needed to manufacture the product (a <u>work order</u>, see page 8)
- <u>how much time</u> should be allowed for each task (use a Gantt chart, see page 8)
- the <u>equipment, labour and materials</u> needed for each stage of production, and the <u>costs</u> of these (use a <u>spreadsheet</u> to work out <u>total costs</u>)
- which <u>members of the team</u> are responsible for completing each task

*Example of a Work Order: Flow Chart for Batch-Producing T-shirts*

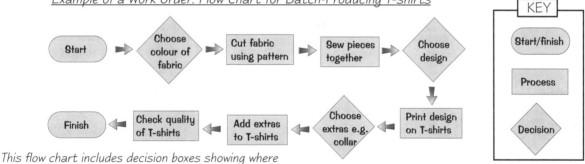

*This flow chart includes decision boxes showing where the design could be varied between batches.*

## Economy of Scale — it's Cheaper to Manufacture in Bulk

The <u>cost</u> of an item gets <u>lower</u> the more of them you produce. This is called <u>economy of scale</u>. So <u>mass-produced products</u> are generally <u>cheaper</u> than one-off products. This is because:

1) Manufacturers of mass-produced or batch-produced products <u>buy materials</u> and extras (e.g. fastenings) in <u>large quantities</u>. They can negotiate <u>discounts</u> because they're buying so much.
2) In mass production, <u>tasks</u> are done <u>repetitively</u> by a worker or machine. This is a <u>quick and efficient</u> way of working — which saves money.
3) Mass production and batch production often use <u>CAD/CAM</u> to control machinery to produce <u>large numbers</u> of <u>identical components</u>. This is a quick, accurate method of production which <u>saves money</u>.

## *Economy of scale — 50 trout skins for a tenner...*

Try making a batch of products using your production plan. Then evaluate how well it worked — could things have gone more smoothly? Improve your production plan, and try again. Practice makes perfect...

# Use of ICT in Your Work

ICT can be used throughout your work to give your project that professional finish.

## The Internet is Great for Research

Using the <u>internet</u>, you can find out information from <u>anywhere in the world</u>.

> **EXAMPLE — Using the Internet to Contact a Manufacturer**
>
> STEP 1: Go to your favourite <u>search engine</u> (e.g. www.google.co.uk or www.yahoo.com)
>
> STEP 2: Type in some <u>keywords</u>. Be <u>specific</u> — if you're looking for leopard-print underwear manufacturers in the Bolton area, you could type "underwear, leopard, Bolton".
>
> STEP 3: When you find a manufacturer, e-mail them your request. <u>Be specific</u> about what you want to find out, they're not mind-readers.

## Use Wordprocessing to Smarten Up Questionnaires and Specifications

A <u>questionnaire</u> is invaluable when you want to ask your target market about a new product. Make an effort and write it out on the <u>computer</u>. It'll be easier to <u>read</u>, you can <u>print out</u> as many as you need, and it'll look <u>neater</u> and more <u>professional</u> which is great for your <u>marks</u>. Doing <u>graphs of your results</u> could add a real wow factor to your research.

Questionnaire

1. Are you male / female ?

2. Which age group are you in?
15-19  20-25  26-old

3. Do you wear underwear?
Yes / No

You can write your <u>specification</u> on the computer too.

* Use <u>bullet points</u>
* to really stress the <u>important points</u>
* just like this.

## Use a Digital Camera, 3D Imaging or a Spreadsheet to Present Your Ideas

1) <u>Scan</u> your ideas/ fabric samples in and make use of a <u>graphics program</u> where you can manipulate <u>colours</u>, <u>shapes</u> and <u>styles</u>.

2) If you have <u>3D CAD</u>, you can even make a <u>3D image</u> of your product, and fit a scanned fabric image onto it.

3) Use a <u>digital camera</u> to make a <u>record</u> of your <u>final ideas</u> or <u>prototype</u>.

4) Use a <u>spreadsheet</u> to work out any <u>costings</u>.

## Computerised Machines Help You Make Your Product

1) A <u>scan and sew</u> machine produces <u>computerised embroidery</u>. As well as using the <u>pre-programmed</u> designs you can use special software to produce <u>your own</u> designs.

2) A <u>plotter and cutter</u> machine can be linked up to a computer, allowing you to produce <u>vinyl iron-on stencils</u> or stencils you can use to add <u>colour</u> to fabric.

3) There are lots of special <u>CAD</u> packages that will enable you to produce <u>paper patterns</u> or find the most economical <u>lay plan</u> (the plan showing how pattern pieces should be cut out of a piece of fabric) for your product.

4) Using <u>CAD/CAM</u> produces the same result time after time. Whatever the ICT opportunities available to you, <u>make the most of them</u>.

## The Internet — useful for much more than just E-bay...

Yep, examiners just love to see computer trickery being used in projects. I think it's because they can't use computers themselves, so they think it's all really impressive — but I know you can do all this stuff in your sleep...

# Use of ICT in Industry

ICT has made textile production loads easier and more flexible. It's used in design, manufacture, quality control and communication — all the stuff that needs to go smoothly for you to end up with a decent product.

## The Internet has had an Impact on the Textiles Industry

1) Textile designers use the Internet as a tool for <u>research</u>.
   By surfing the web they can look for <u>new trends</u> and <u>design inspiration</u>.

2) Manufacturers use the Internet for <u>market research</u>, e.g. finding out information about competitors' <u>products</u> and <u>sales figures</u>. This information is used for <u>forecasting new trends</u>, identifying <u>gaps in the product range</u> and <u>spotting gaps in the market</u> for new products.

3) <u>E-mail</u> is used by manufacturers to <u>contact consumers</u>, e.g. sending out <u>questionnaires</u> to find out more about the people buying the products, and sending out <u>advertising promotions</u> about new products.

4) E-mail has also enabled <u>remote working</u>. This means different members of a <u>team</u> are able to <u>work far apart</u> — but <u>communicate</u> ideas, designs and information <u>quickly</u> via e-mail. This is very useful for <u>multi-national companies</u> which have bases in several countries.

## Computer-Aided Design (CAD) is Used by Textile Designers

CAD has revolutionized the way textile products are <u>designed</u> in industry. Four main uses of CAD are:

1) The production of <u>mood boards</u>, <u>designs</u>, <u>3D images</u> and <u>virtual catwalks</u> by a designer to present their ideas to clients and manufacturers — and to quickly <u>adapt</u> and <u>modify</u> them as necessary.

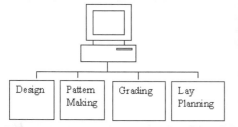

2) Designing <u>textile patterns</u>.

3) Calculating how to change a pattern to make <u>different sizes</u> of garment (this is called '<u>grading</u>').

4) Deciding the <u>pattern lay</u> (where the different pattern pieces will be cut out of the fabric) on-screen. It's important to get this right so <u>fabric isn't wasted</u>.

## Computers are Used to Make Production More Efficient

<u>Computers</u> are used to <u>control many operations</u> in a textile factory.
Using computers to help with production is called <u>Computer-Aided Manufacture</u>.

1) Computers can be used to <u>monitor</u> and <u>control</u> parts of the <u>manufacturing process</u>, e.g. the amount, weight and thickness of <u>materials</u>, the <u>time</u> a process lasts for and the <u>temperature</u>.

2) <u>Data</u> can be downloaded from <u>CAD/CAM software</u> on a computer to a <u>CNC manufacturing machine</u> — to accurately control the way the machine processes material (see page 22).
   Examples of <u>CNC machines</u> used in the textile industry are:
   • The <u>POEM embroidery machine</u> which is used to accurately reproduce badges and logos.
   • The <u>CAMM1 cutter and plotter</u> which is used for making stencils.

3) CAM is really useful for <u>batch production</u>, e.g. fabric is cut out using <u>computer-controlled cutters</u> that cut through several layers of fabric at once — producing a <u>batch</u> of <u>identical fabric pieces</u>.
   <u>New instructions</u> can be downloaded to the machines when a batch of <u>different</u> sized pieces is needed.

## Designers communicate via e-mail — or textile messages...

You should definitely be familiar with all this CAD/CAM stuff now, and I bet you use the Internet all the time. The important thing now is to apply all that stuff to the way it's used in industry.

# People Involved in Textile Products

The life of a textile product involves a chain of people from Client to Customer. Read on.

## The Client is Whoever's Asked You to Make the Product

- You need to find out <u>who</u> your client is, and what their <u>needs</u> and <u>wants</u> are for a new textile product.

- You could do this by asking them questions in the form of a <u>questionnaire</u>.
  You could look at relevant <u>books</u>, the <u>internet</u> or <u>past trends</u> for your target market.

- You need to make sure any information is <u>relevant</u>
  to your project and what your client wants.

## The Designer Designs the Product

- <u>Designers</u> in large textiles companies have to work within various <u>restrictions</u>.

- You'll have been informed who your client (target market) is and what they want.

- Your company wants to make <u>money</u> so there will be <u>restrictions</u> on the amount the <u>fabric</u> and <u>components</u> you use on products. Your company may have their <u>own fabrics</u> you have to use.

- You need to consider how <u>long</u> production will take
  (<u>time is money</u> — if production takes too long then you'll make no profit).

*(And that's all before you even start designing.)*

## Manufacturers Make the Product

- <u>Manufacturers</u> are the people who <u>make</u> the products.

- They want and need to make a <u>profit</u>, and will do everything they can to <u>make sure</u> this happens.

- They calculate their costs in two ways:
  <u>DIRECT</u> — *these are the actual costs that occur during manufacture.*
  <u>INDIRECT</u> — *things like running machines, and the costs of planning and design.*

- The manufacturer will make sure they have the right people <u>trained</u> to do the jobs.
  Many workers are <u>multi-skilled</u> so that they can replace people who are sick or on holiday.

## Customers Buy and Use the Product

- <u>Customers</u> are the people who <u>use</u> the product.

- Customers go to a shop, <u>buy</u> the product, take it home and <u>use</u> it. If it <u>doesn't work</u>,
  or <u>falls apart</u> after the first wash, they'll probably take it back to the shop and <u>COMPLAIN</u>.

- It's up to the <u>manufacturer</u> to get the product right first time to <u>avoid</u>
  any complaints and fulfil the <u>customer's expectation</u> of the product.

- Some high street stores are regarded as having a <u>high customer satisfaction</u>
  and pride themselves on their <u>reputation</u> for good quality products.

## *We're in the middle of a chain reaction...*

Repeat it like a mantra — client, designer, manufacturer, customer (or my handy acronym: CoDMuC).
Then learn all the details for each bit of the textile product chain.

# Advertising and Marketing

*I've made my products, I've put them in a box under the bed, I've kept it a big secret, I'm expecting to sell loads...* [I'm a fool.]

## Advertise and Market Your Product, Otherwise it Won't Sell

Once a product has been designed and made, it has to be <u>sold</u>. A manufacturer will <u>promote</u> their products by <u>marketing</u>.

Marketing is about <u>setting prices</u> people will want to pay, <u>promoting</u> the product and finding a <u>suitable place</u> to sell the product.

Major companies spend *<u>LOADS OF MONEY</u>* on <u>advertising</u> their products. Places you can advertise include:

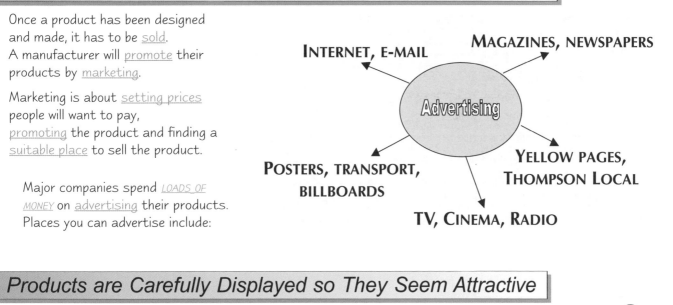

INTERNET, E-MAIL

MAGAZINES, NEWSPAPERS

**Advertising**

POSTERS, TRANSPORT, BILLBOARDS

YELLOW PAGES, THOMPSON LOCAL

TV, CINEMA, RADIO

## Products are Carefully Displayed so They Seem Attractive

1) Products are put in <u>shop windows</u> to encourage customers to come inside.

2) Once inside, customers find the products <u>grouped</u> by design or maybe colour.

3) <u>Furnishings</u> are displayed in a <u>room setting</u> to make them look <u>attractive</u>.

4) <u>Outfits</u> are displayed on <u>mannequins</u> to make them <u>look good</u>. *The aim is to make customers think that <u>they</u> will <u>look good too</u> if they buy the clothes.*

*Which dress would you rather buy?*

## Shops Aim Their Advertising and Marketing at Their Shoppers

Shops <u>aim</u> their advertising and marketing at <u>their own target market</u>. *For example, some high street stores target a specific age group (e.g. Tammy Girl, aimed at teenage girls).*

Department stores tend to sell a <u>range</u> of products to a <u>variety</u> of customers. <u>Each department</u> will be aimed at a <u>different</u> target market.

<u>Boutiques</u> are more <u>exclusive</u>, selling high fashion garments that are usually more expensive.

<u>Supermarkets</u> jumped on the clothing band wagon a few years ago — most of the major ones have a fashion department. They're targeting <u>shoppers</u> as they do their <u>weekly shop</u>.

<u>Mail order companies</u> produce <u>catalogues</u> with <u>glossy pictures</u> to make their products look attractive. Both <u>traditional</u> mail order companies and <u>internet</u> companies are targeted at the <u>home shopper</u> — they work hard to make the shopping process <u>simple and easy</u>.

## *I still can't quite get my head around buying jeans at Asda...*

It's all very well designing and making the best floral-print boiler suit ever, but you'll never make any money if you don't let people know that they can buy one. Then again, the advance orders haven't exactly been pouring in...

# Revision Summary

*OK, you've read the section — now it's time to prove you've learnt the lesson.*
*You have one minute (well, about half an hour or so) to answer questions on your chosen specialist subject;*
*TEXTILES: Design and Market Influences. If you don't know an answer, you may say 'pass' (and then go back and*
*look it up in the section). Any questions? No? Then your time starts... now...*

1) When conducting product analysis, list eight things you should consider about the product.
2) In terms of design: What is 'ambience'?
    What is 'harmony'?
3) List three types of colour harmony.
4) Suggest why a company might use bright colours when designing its uniforms, logos and interiors.
5) What is a prototype?
6) Explain what the following terms mean: a) Quality Assurance; b) Quality Control.
7) List three benefits that a company would gain from having a good system of quality control.
8) Suggest five sources of information you could use to conduct research into the needs of your target market.
9) List three factors that can affect what people choose to buy, other than fashion trends.
10) What does the Trades Description Act prevent manufacturers doing?
11) Under the Supply of Goods Act 1979, what three criteria must mail-order goods fulfil?
12) What does it mean when a product displays this symbol?

13) Suggest three things you could do to make operating machinery safer.
14) List five things you should consider about the environment in which your product will be made.
15) Under the Health and Safety at Work Act, what must a business do before it begins production?
16) List four ways in which the textiles industry harms the environment.
17) What are pinking shears?
18) List three ways that you can stop the edges of your fabric fraying.
19) What does it mean if an industrial sewing machine is described as 'multi-headed'?
20) One-off production is more expensive than mass production. Why would anyone choose to use it?
21) Describe how 'In-line production' works.
22) List three advantages of using a 'Just-in-time' system of supply.
23) List four advantages of using CAM.
24) A company makes embroidered baseball caps. Suggest two possible inputs, two possible transformations, and two possible outputs for their system of production.
25) What is a sub assembly? Give an example.
26) List five things that your production plan should include.
27) Describe how 'economy of scale' works.
28) List four ways in which computers can assist you in your design and production process.
29) List four ways in which CAD/CAM can speed up production and reduce waste in the textiles industry.
30) What are 'direct costs' of manufacture? What are 'indirect costs'?
31) Explain how shops display textiles products in order to make them more appealing to the customer.

# Tips on Getting Started

This section's got all the stuff people <u>don't</u> do that the examiners get really annoyed about.
Read this before you start your project to make sure you keep those markers happy.

## Step 1 — Get your Idea

You can get ideas from <u>different</u> places — for example, your teacher might:

1) <u>tell</u> you exactly what your task is.

2) give you a <u>range</u> of different tasks to choose from.

3) leave the project <u>choice</u> completely up to you.

## Don't choose anything Too Easy or Too Boring

Choose a project that will:

1) <u>stretch</u> you and let you <u>demonstrate</u> just how <u>good</u> you are. If the project's too <u>easy</u>, or contains little scope for design, then you'll <u>lose</u> valuable marks.

2) be <u>interesting</u> and <u>challenging</u> enough to keep you <u>motivated</u>. Coursework's a <u>long</u> old process and you need to stay <u>committed</u>.

3) give you the opportunity to produce a <u>wide range</u> of <u>research</u> and demonstrate your <u>ICT</u> skills.

4) allow for a <u>variety</u> of solutions, resulting in <u>one</u> which can be completed <u>before the</u> <u>deadline</u> (and this includes allowing time for <u>testing</u> and <u>evaluation</u> to take place).

## The Design Brief — Give Loads of Detail

1) Your idea needs to have "<u>real commercial potential</u>".

2) You need to describe <u>exactly</u> what you're trying to do.

3) <u>Explain all the factors</u> you need to consider — things like price, weight, market trends, etc.

> See page 1 for more on the design brief.

## Say Why your Research is Relevant

1) <u>DON'T</u> just <u>plonk</u> bits of paper in your research folder without any explanation.

2) <u>DON'T</u> just copy and paste stuff from the net either.

3) <u>DO</u> <u>write notes</u> on <u>every</u> piece of research to say <u>why</u> it's <u>relevant</u>, how it changed your thinking or how it backed up your existing ideas.

4) <u>DO</u> <u>refer back</u> to the research section <u>throughout the project</u> — it shows the markers that you've <u>used your research</u>.

> See page 2 for more on research.

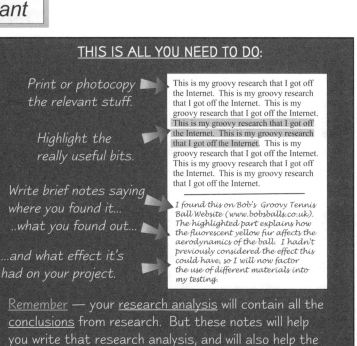

**THIS IS ALL YOU NEED TO DO:**

*Print or photocopy the relevant stuff.*

This is my groovy research that I got off the Internet. This is my groovy research that I got off the Internet. This is my groovy research that I got off the Internet. This is my groovy research that I got off the Internet. This is my groovy research that I got off the Internet. This is my groovy research that I got off the Internet. This is my groovy research that I got off the Internet. This is my groovy research that I got off the Internet.

*Highlight the really useful bits.*

I found this on Bob's Groovy Tennis Ball Website (www.bobsballs.co.uk). The highlighted part explains how the fluorescent yellow fur affects the aerodynamics of the ball. I hadn't previously considered the effect this could have, so I will now factor the use of different materials into my testing.

*Write brief notes saying where you found it...*
*...what you found out...*
*...and what effect it's had on your project.*

<u>Remember</u> — your <u>research analysis</u> will contain all the <u>conclusions</u> from research. But these notes will help you write that research analysis, and will also help the examiner understand why you made your decisions.

# Tips on Development

If you're smart, you'll keep planning and evaluating throughout your project. If you're a <u>buffoon</u>, you'll do a bit at the start, then forget about it and get a bad mark for your project.

## You Need a Wide Range of Ideas — Be Creative

1) There's more than one way to <u>skin a cat</u>.
2) Consider <u>plenty</u> of <u>different ways</u> to <u>solve</u> the problem.
3) <u>Don't</u> just come up with <u>one good idea</u> and stick with it.
   You'll only be sure it's the <u>best</u> idea if you've <u>thought about other ways</u> of doing it.
4) The examiners do really get <u>annoyed</u> about this one —
   so get those creative juices flowing.

## Developing your Ideas — Try Out a Few Alternatives

1) The same goes for <u>developing</u> ideas as for <u>creating</u> them.
2) There's still <u>more than one</u> way to skin a cat.
3) Once you've got the idea, there are still <u>plenty</u> of ways to turn that into an <u>ace product</u>.

## Do Loads of Planning — and Not Just at the Start

Planning is for life, not just for... um... the start of your project.
These are the things you should do:

### OVERALL PROJECT PLAN AT THE START:

1) to help you <u>focus</u> on the task
2) to make sure you know what stage you should have reached at various times — this way, if you fall behind schedule, you'll know about it as soon as possible, and can <u>do something about it</u>
3) to allow enough time for <u>all</u> the different stages of the design process — including testing, evaluation, and writing up your project

Remember to include testing and evaluating in your time plan — it's all too easy to forget them...

### PLAN YOUR RESEARCH:

Work out what <u>research</u> you need to do, and how long you're going to allow yourself for each bit (e.g. questionnaires, disassembling a similar product, and so on).

### DON'T GET BOGGED DOWN:

When you're generating proposals or developing your product, don't spend too long working on <u>one little aspect</u> of the product. There's a lot to do — so try to keep your project <u>moving forward</u>.

## I have a cunning plan...

OK, repeat after me: "I will allow time for testing in my time plan. I will allow time for testing in my time plan. I will allow time for testing in my time plan. I will allow time for testing in my time plan..."

# Tips on Evaluation

<u>Evaluation</u> means <u>examining</u> and <u>judging</u> your work (and <u>you</u> have to do this as part of your project — it's not just something for the examiner to do). If your product doesn't work, but you explain <u>why</u>, you can still get <u>good marks</u>.

## Test and Evaluate your Product Throughout the Project

I quote:

> *"To be achieving the highest marks in this section, candidates must show
> that they have used a clear and objective testing strategy."*

That's from one of the Chief Examiners' Reports.
(In other words, it's <u>really important</u> that you keep testing and evaluating your work all through the project.)

## Don't Wait until you're Finished to Evaluate your Work

1) Like any designer, it's a good idea to be thinking about <u>evaluation</u>
   from the moment you <u>start</u> working on your <u>design brief</u>.

2) Make <u>notes</u> on your <u>designs</u> and <u>developments</u> as you go along,
   explaining what was <u>good</u> and <u>bad</u> about each one.

3) When you're writing up your <u>final evaluation</u>, you can also think about whether you'd
   do anything <u>differently</u> if you were starting again. It's okay if you made some <u>bad
   decisions</u> during your project — everyone does. But you can get marks if you
   <u>explain why</u> they were bad decisions, and what you <u>wish</u> you'd done instead.

## Check your Brief and Specification

You need to evaluate your product <u>fully</u>. Use these guidelines:

1) <u>Compare</u> your final product to your <u>brief</u> and <u>specification</u>. Does your product
   satisfy all the conditions it's supposed to? If not, why not?

2) Try to get a <u>likely user</u> (or an expert in this kind of product, maybe) to <u>trial</u> your product and give
   their <u>honest opinions</u>. This will give you a <u>realistic view</u> of whether it's <u>fit for its purpose</u>
   — e.g. does it do what it is meant to? And if it does, how well? They may also be able to give
   you ideas for possible improvements.

3) It's dead important to think about possible <u>improvements</u> you could make as well, such as...

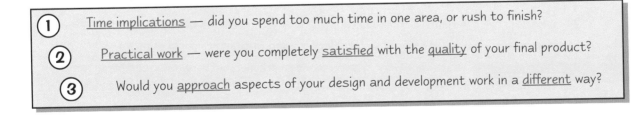

    (1)    <u>Time implications</u> — did you spend too much time in one area, or rush to finish?

    (2)    <u>Practical work</u> — were you completely <u>satisfied</u> with the <u>quality</u> of your final product?

    (3)    Would you <u>approach</u> aspects of your design and development work in a <u>different</u> way?

## <u>Never forget to check your briefs...</u>

Everyone makes mistakes (well, everyone except me, obviously). More specifically, everyone makes mistakes in their
D & T projects. So don't worry too much when it happens to you.
Just explain what went wrong and how you'd avoid it in the future. You can get marks for that.

# Presentation

It's no use doing a stonking project if your presentation's naff. You've put a lot of time and effort into your project (probably) so it would be a shame for you to mess it up at the last stage.

### *IT REALLY IS WORTH PUTTING IN THOSE FEW EXTRA HOURS.*

## The Finished Product — Good Photographs are Ace

Your evaluation should be <u>clearly presented</u> and <u>easy to read</u>.

1) Include an introduction to give a bit of <u>background information</u> — e.g. how you came to think of the project.

2) Always take photos of any <u>non-permanent</u> work or <u>intermediate stages</u> in making the product. You can use either a <u>normal</u> or a <u>digital camera</u> and then either <u>glue in</u> the print or <u>place</u> the digital image into a word-processed document — whatever suits.

> Photos are the only way of getting a lasting record of your work — and the examiners *REALLY WANT* you to do it.

3) Use a <u>mixture of media</u> to present your project. It's always good to <u>show off</u> how nifty you are with CAD or that desktop publishing program, but don't forget about <u>old-fashioned words</u> to explain what you did, and <u>sketches</u> and <u>prototypes</u> to show how you did it.

4) Split up your evaluation into <u>different sections</u> to make it easy to read. Give each section a <u>clear heading</u>.

The sections could include:
a) how well your product satisfies the brief and specification
b) results from user trials
c) problems you encountered
d) improvements for the future

5) Think about how it fits together — your project needs to work <u>as a whole</u>. It should flow <u>seamlessly</u> from one bit to the next — don't just shove loads of separate bits in with no clue as to how they fit together.

## Vocabulary — use the Right Technical Terms

### BIG, FANCY WORDS:

1) Do yourself a favour — <u>learn all the technical terms</u> relevant to your subject.
2) And how to <u>spell</u> them.
3) And don't worry if you sound <u>poncy</u>.
4) Using the right technical terms <u>impresses the examiners</u>. They say so in their reports.

### GRAMMAR, SPELLING, PUNCTUATION:

1) Treat your project like an <u>English essay</u>.
2) Get your <u>spellings</u> right. Double-check any words you often get wrong.
3) Remember to use full stops and capital letters and write in <u>proper sentences</u>.
4) <u>Short sentences</u> make your work clearer. Long sentences, with loads of commas, can often get very confusing, because it's easy, once you get to the end of the sentence, to forget what you were reading right at the start.
5) Structure your work in <u>paragraphs</u> — a new paragraph for a new topic.

## <u>Santa cheats at presentation — he uses elves...</u>

Of course your project has to look nice. I mean, what would you rather read... a beautifully presented folder of work, or something scribbled down on the back of a mucky paper towel...

# Summary Checklist

This stuff can really make your project _sparkle_.
That's why I've given it a whole extra page — so you can't forget <u>any</u> of it.
Before you hand in your project, make sure you've covered all of these bits,
and you'll be well on your way to D & T heaven.

## Sparkly Project Checklist

☐ 1) My design brief has got loads of detail.

☐ 2) I've done plenty of research, and said why it's relevant.

☐ 3) I've made a detailed design specification.

☐ 4) I've come up with a wide range of project proposals.

☐ 5) I've included different ways of developing my product, and explained why I made my decisions.

☐ 6) I've tested my product on consumers.

7) I've done loads of planning, including:

    ☐ a) a production plan (time plan),

    ☐ b) planning for mass production.

☐ 8) I've evaluated my product throughout the project.

☐ 9) I've taken photos of everything that won't last.

☐ 10) I've used a mixture of media to present my project.

☐ 11) I've checked my spelling and grammar.

☐ 12) I've used the right technical terms.

# Index

# Index

# Index